ABYEI

REPEATED HISTORY
OF EXCLUSION
& POLITICAL DERELICTION

The Story of How
The Abyei Political Question
was Ignominiously Shunned

Jok Alor Bulabek

Cover design, typesetting and layout: Africa World Books
Unit 3, 57 Frobisher St, Osborne Park, WA 6017
P.O. Box 1106 Osborne Park, WA 6916

Africa
World Books
Pty Ltd

To Ngok's women throughout history up to the present date: your sacrifices and contributions are of inestimable value. Your position in the struggle has never gone unnoticed. Thanks a million.

CONTENTS

Dedication   *ix*

Acronyms   *xi*

Acknowledgements   *xv*

Foreword   *xix*

Author's Memoir   *xxi*

Part 1: The Genesis of The Abyei Political Question 1

1. A Solution Turned into a Problem   3

Part 2: Abyei; A Case of Political Dereliction   15

2. Ngok: The Gate Guarders   17

3. Abyei from Addis Ababa to Machakos   24

4. Khartoum's Deviational Stratagem   29

5. Abyei's Invasion   34

Part 3: The Perturbation   51

6. The Fake Hope   53

7. Abyei Community's Referendum   65

8. Reactions on Abyei Community's Referendum   70

Part 4: Post-Bellum South Sudan   77

9. The Ephemeral Joy   79

10. SPLM'S Infighting Impact on Abyei   86

Part 5: Left In The Lurch   95

11. Sold Out in the Eleventh Hour!   97

12. A Henchman was Found   107

13. Attacks on Aneet   123

14. Was Hussein Suited to the Mission?   129

15. The Second Wave of Attacks   144

16. Was the Conflict Preventable?   159

Part 6: Revivification of Ngok-Twic Relations   171

17. Ngok and Kuac throughout history   173

18. Yestern's brothers turned enemies today   180

19. Was it really between Twic and Ngok?   190

Part 7: The Unfinished Mission   197

20. The Fate of a Mis-Negotiated Deal   199

Appendix   *207*

Abyei's people did not join the Anya-nya Movements and Sudan People's Liberation Army to be lesser Southerners.

The spirits of Ngok's fallen heroes who made ultimate sacrifices for South Sudan to exist, shall never rest in peace, until Abyei is back to South Sudan.

What affected the issue of Abyei was not only NCP's intransigent political position, but Kiir Administration's oscillating policies too.

To nosey parkers who have been exacerbating the conflict between Ngok and Twic, stop your meddlesome predilection! You don't know how mixed is the blood of Twic and Ngok.

The common interest for the communities of Twic and Ngok is peace, anyone found flying against, must be cast out, and considered a strange bird.

Real heroes and heroines are those who win the battle of peacemaking, their beneficence lasts for ages.

DEDICATION

This book is dedicated to Ngok heroes throughout history up to recent martyrs of Tiit-Bai whose sacrifices embodied the real meaning of intrepidity and altruism; my cousin Alor Miyen Bulabek who demised in mysterious circumstances during the struggle; my father, a friend and a mentor whose image shall indelibly remain in my mind; an amiable human, Deng Arop Deng Kuol, and my 7-day-old firstborn to whom I gave no name then, but today 26 May 2024, after twenty years, I decided to posthumously give him my name. When I lost him, I felt a piece of me was taken. Respects to all of them in their glorious, transcendental paradise of righteousness.

ACRONYMS

AAA: Abyei Administrative Area

ABC: Abyei Boundaries Commission

ACAD: Abyei's Community Action for Development

AFFC: Aneet Facts Finding Committee

AJOC: Abyei Joint Oversight Committee

ALF: Abyei Liberation Front

ASAA: Abyei Special Administrative Area

AU: African Union

AUC: African Union Commission

AUHIP: African Union High Implementation Panel

AUPSC: African Union Peace and Security Council

CA: Chief Administrator

CoHA: Cessation of Hostilities Agreement

CPA: Comprehensive Peace Agreement

G10: A political group comprising 10 members, also known as Former Detainees

G13: A group of 13 Volunteers that initiated the Abyei Communal Referendum

GANBATT: Ghanaian Battalion in the United Nations Interim Force for Abyei

GoS: Government of Sudan

GoSS: Government of South/ern Sudan

IDPs: Internally Displaced Persons

IGAD: Inter-Governmental Authority on Development

INDBATT: Indian Battalion in the United Nations Interim Force for Abyei

J1: A residential area in Juba where South Sudan State's House is located

JCE: Jieng Council of Elders

JEM: Justice and Equality Movement

JIU: Joint Integrated Unit

NCP: National Congress Party

NLC: National Liberation Council

PCA: Permanent Court of Arbitration

PDF: Popular Defense Force

QIP: Quick Impact Project

R_ARCISS: Revitalized Agreement on the Resolution of Conflict in South Sudan

RPG: Rocket Propelled Grenade

R_TNLA: Revitalized Transitional National Legislative Assembly

RSF: Rapid Support Force

SAF: Sudanese Armed Forces

SCP: Sudanese Communist Party

SF: Southern Front

SPLA: Sudan People's Liberation Army
SPLM: Sudan People's Liberation Movement
SSPM: South Sudan People's Movement
SSPDF: South Sudan People's Defense Force
SSTV: South Sudan Television
TB: Tiit-Bai / Abyei Home Guards
UDF: United Democratic Front
UDSF: United Democratic Salvation Front
UNISFA: United Nations Interim Security Force for Abyei
UNMISS: United Nations Mission in South Sudan
VoA: Voice of America
VP: Vice President

ACKNOWLEDGEMENTS

As someone who was born and grew up in war-effected dehumanising circumstances in Abyei up to the mid-1980s, it would be preternatural not to be preoccupied with politics. My childhood's memory is full of traumatic incidents and indelible voices which are still boisterously clanging at the posterior part of my head. Those circumstances made up the very person I am today—words such as Jur, Jung e Jur and Jamil (Arab, Horse and Camel) were anxiously and fearfully pronounced daily.

These abysmal episodes had unfortunately been repeated shortly after South Sudan's independence, when civil war broke out in 2013. I was less affected personally, compared to how it was in Abyei in the '80s, but seeing pictures of terrified mothers tying kids at their backs, carrying stuff on their heads, reawakened the grief of the traumatised child in me. In fact, I did not expect to see the same gruesome agonising pictures of destruction and death caused by folks of our own kindred! People were completely down in the mouth, predators who had been mostly in uniform, this time, were our own brethren, Dinkas, Nuers, Shuluks, Equations etc.

For me, writing a book had been an *idée fixe*, particularly, about Abyei's political question, but time was not fixed, until two things transpired; Twic instigated against Ngok, attacked Aneet on 10 February 2022, and my conscience-driven resignation from SPLM /IO and the Revitalised Transitional National Legislative Assembly (R_TNLA) in October 2022. Though I managed to put on a brave face, both events were hard to deal with. Therefore, it was advisable not to be effusive. In such circumstances, one must find something objective to engage oneself with, in order to avoid any probable negativity. Then came the idea of a long- thought about project—authoring a book.

With this experience, I recognised the pithy saying that positivity is acquirable, and that optimism incurs positivism. When you keep around you people with optimistic ideas, they would possibly affect and infect you, hence your thoughts could turn positive. Thanks to my comrades in Abyei's Voice for Security and Stability (AVSS), for their moral support, sincere advice and encouragement. I would also like to recognise Kuol D. Kuol's rational guidance, and Giir M. Alie's invaluable consolation which calmed me down when I was feeling a bit restless. Having such awesome people around me during those stressful moments was really a blessing.

Great appreciation goes to my family members, particularly, immediate dependents who innocently bore the brunt of my often-venturesome decisions, Special gratitude in this regard is owed to my elder daughters Akuet and Achai, who despite the extreme impact of my decisions on them, did not complain, and their patience remains my source of inspiration. I am profoundly grateful to Paramount Chief of Ngok Dinka of Abyei, Bulabek Deng Kuol, Chief Akonon Ajuong Deng Tiel of Anyiel Chieftaincy and Chief Arop Kuol Kon Tingloth of Diil Chieftaincy for their valued information, particularly history of relations between Ngok and Twic. Not forgetting the most important respondents, elder Anie Ajak Malual (Ajak Wun-Kur) and Cok Deng Kuol (Deng-Makuei) for their noteworthy, historical narratives about relations between Ngok and Misseriya.

Last but not least, I would love to thank anyone who provided me with a piece of information, Mithiang Wour, Francis Mayik, Bol B. Bol, Aguer Nyok Bar, Deng Kiir Mater, Mayol Deng Dau Dhal and Madam Buthina Saeed, your contributions were really of inestimable value. Likewise, appreciation goes to Daniel Alor Miyen who ably did accurate observations on the manuscript which I took to heart. Finally, I would like to deeply thank Mr. Akol Miyen Kuol for the eloquently written foreword and factual review of the script.

For those who may feel censured, whether Ngok leaders of the SPLM, Twic members of National Legislature, or South Sudan's most senior citizens, uncle Bona Malwal Madut and President Salva Kiir Mayardit, I would like to declare that I hold no personal grudge against anyone. It's all about public matters.

FOREWORD

I hope I will not be exaggerating if I say that, *Abyei: Repeated History of Exclusion and Political Dereliction*, is the most moving and authoritative book I have ever read on the controversy surrounding the fate of Abyei, the home territory of the nine Ngok Dinka Chiefdoms.

Abyei - a region that is the size of Jamaica - straddles the border between South Sudan and Sudan, and it is rich with water, wildlife, forestry, livestock, fishery, oil, and most importantly, a vast fertile land for agriculture.

Furthermore, the native Ngok Dinka, are highly educated people. Sadly, they have been unable to fully employ their acquired knowledge and experience in various fields and demonstrate their abilities, skills and talents due to the undecided future status of their region.

The author Jok Alor Bulabek's style of writing is very beautiful, straight-forward and captures the attention of the reader, especially the way he narrated the historical background of Abyei Region and what his Ngok Dinka people have gone through throughout history and the indifference of both countries—Sudan and South Sudan— to determine the final status of his home region.

Reading this beautiful book with the author's interesting approach to the long-standing issue, is like watching a movie. The author Jok has stated very clearly and frankly, in the book, how Abyei found itself in this dilemma and who are behind the undecided status of this strategic and rich region.

Hence, it is my great pleasure to recommend this unique book to all the children of Abyei and all those interested in history and learning about the determination of a people who are ready to fight to the end to liberate their homeland and safeguard its border from any external aggression.

Akol Miyen Kuol,
Author, Poet and Analyst,
Nairobi, KENYA,
25 January 2025

AUTHOR'S MEMOIR

I was born in Abyei-Nai Nai village, in approximately 1977. There were neither hospitals nor health centres, like all the marginalised areas in the quondam Sudan's Southern region where people until recent times continued to live in unendurable conditions. Nai-Nai is the cradle home where my umbilical cord was buried. Like any agrarian community, it was predominantly inhabited by one family: Bulabek Biong's and his brother Leng Biong's extended families. It later became known as Nai-nai Pan Acuil Wunbiong. Acuil Bulabek Biong was the first Chief for Abior chieftaincy. This, of course, didn't make it their exclusive residence. Some other families were sharing them.

For Abyei area, the late 1960s were disastrous. The area lost its visionary and charismatic leader Deng Kuol Arop (Deng Majok) in September 1969. He died in a critical time when the relation between Ngok and Misseriya reached its peak of pugnacity and the power equation had already begun to lose its balance. It was the same decade when Sudan's Central Government conspicuously intensified its support to Misseriya against Ngok and other bordering communities. There were so many catastrophic political developments to mention; the horrendous assassination of Anyiel Kuol Arop who was seated at his yard in Mading-Thon and shot by government forces. Death took the Paramount Chief Deng Majok when Ngok needed his presence more than ever. His death left a vacuum, exactly like when SPLM lost Dr. John Garang de Mabior.

I cannot clearly retrieve the events of those days, but sharply as children's memories, I'm still keeping some pictures of the mid-1980s when most of Ngok's villages were displaced, except Abyei town plus a few thorps fearfully inhabited due to the extent of the violence. The displacement campaign was directly launched by the 31st infamous Brigade of the Sudanese Armed Forces of Hajana Western Division based in Abyei. This Brigade remained in Abyei until substituted with JIUs after the May 2008 incident. Together with others, my family moved to Minyang Anyiel and took refuge in aunt Adhat Bulabek Biong's house, stayed for some time then we proceeded up to Mareng Diil which is my maternal uncle's home. We resided in Rum- loom when first hosted by uncle Bol Kooryuek from Padool Dill clan before Father bartered a plot with a she-cow. In Mareng Diil we also witnessed abhorrent times when some factions of Bul Nuer started aggressive attacks on Diil Chieftaincy.

Despite all these traumatising circumstances, my memory keeps at the surface some worthy images. I was sometimes assigned to look after calves and goats in the surroundings and also participate in cleaning the byres from the dung. At sunset, when big boys returned the cows, cow-chip was burned to chase away mosquitoes and other insects, these were the kind of duties lads and sometimes lasses were early trained to do. I also remember the names of a few dignitaries from the Anyar Diil age-set which is the counter age-group to my father, Nyang-Ateir-dit Abior, names such as Mangar Ayom, Nyok Bar, Dau Kooryuek, Miyen Kwaja and Mithiang Kuol Monyjok.

The security situation continued to deteriorate in the whole Abyei area and mass migration was the only defining factor of that period. Some migrated towards the south to areas of Twic, Apuk, Abiem in eastern Awiel and some made it up to Luac-jang in Tonj East, but the majority were scattered in many northern states. Father decided to take us to the north because some family members were already in Shendi. Father had two wives, Alek Malith Dau Mijok, my biological mother and Ateng Kwaja Wun-Aceng my stepmother, from Diil's subsections of Paguiny/ Jeglei and Paqueng/Mareng Diil respectively.

On our way back to Abyei, we stopped again at auntie Adhiat's house in Minyang Anyiel. Though she was not at home, we were nicely welcomed by uncle Makor Dheil Deng Piok, an amiable man who had friendly relation with his in-law, Alor Bulabek Biong (my father). We stayed for a period not less than a year, I remember when we were assigned to chase away birds from the farm. One day I unveiled my restive temperament and refused to do the job because we were prevented from eating canes. Elders kept telling us that we should wait for thanksgiving ceremony (Amiyoc-Piny), until crops be graced first by Malualdit (Totem) who was claimed to be the owner of the farm. I then said, "It is fine, but let Malualdit chase the birds away from his farm." Due to that defiant tendency, we won an exemption and were allowed to eat canes (Bel).

Shortly, we left for Abyei after receiving the bad news of my paternal grandmother Nyankiir Ajiing Deng's death. She died and was buried in Abyei Town before news reached us in Minyang Anyiel. Communication was not easy in those days. In Abyei, Father carried out some rituals by sacrificing an old she-cow at his mother's grave according to tradition. After he showed respect to his mother, he decided to take us to Northern Sudan.

We boarded a lorry from Abyei that evening. I was wearing a new jalabiya made from cotton (Damoria). As the lorry drove for some time, we passed through forests, and later reached sandy areas (Agooth / Gooz) where the lorry stopped at some stations. On the way, some people identified their cows which had been raided as we passed by Misseriya's cattle camps along the road. In one of the stations, the driver overstayed inexcusably, and adults were murmuring. Suddenly, a fox came closer and cried, a sign believed to have been a relief, then I saw Father stood away from us, uttering some words to himself. He was praying to ancestors.

Thank God we reached Khartoum safely. In Arabi Market, the downtown area of Khartoum, I drank soda for the first time, an experience I will never forget. When gas went through my nose, I surprisingly cried like a newborn infant. That experience served as an official baptism into townish life. We stayed for some days in Haj Yusif block (5) in the house of late beloved cousin Musa Ringdit Acuil Wunbiong, and after that we proceeded to Shendi. I was taken to school that same year of 1986, thanks to cousin

Cier Agon Arop Biong who took my hand to Shendi Al-Junubia Primary School. Below are some of my school mates: Mayol Deng Dau Dahl, Kuol Akuei, Bol Bulabek, Monywiir Bol Agon Arop and Anyiel Ador Nyinkuany Dau.

I was hairy and a bit light skinned, and one day Madam Igbal Hassan, our Primary (1) Teacher of arithmetic innocently inquired if I am from Misseriya. I became enraged and felt doubly humiliated because Misseriyafor me are enemies. I referred it to my father who was furious and wanted to see that teacher until he was calmed down by some educated young adults in the family. This was, of course, a result of a trauma which many generations share with me and shall indelibly remain for our lifetime. I don't want to be seen here as someone blowing his own trumpet, but I was earning distinctions at school, as many of my cohort in Shendi can attest. I maintained that level despite the hardships, until I finished University of Juba (UoJ) with Bachelor's Degree in Arts and Humanities, Department of Philosophy with Division Two Upper which later qualified me for teaching in the University of Rumbek's College of Education as Teaching Assistant (TA).

Like many of our generation, I was politically pre-oriented as we were staying in communities where SPLA's victories were joyfully celebrated and people followed eagerly SPLA's radio programs, though it was perilous. I consciously grew up knowing that there were people fighting on our behalf in Southern Sudan. When the peace agreement was signed (CPA), I was already a young adult, so I ebulliently enrolled in the political activities. We organised the community and I was selected to chair the SPLM office in Al-Bagier. Together with comrades James Makur Mading Maker,

Dawood Saqiir Shaaib, Simon Deng Tung, Late Peter Geleng, Ahmed Daldom, Zeinab Musa, Ibrahim Noreen, Abuk Deng Guem, Ali Mustafa Tiia, Omar Musa Tagiel, Joseph Malual, Joseph Achiery, Chol Mawiew Chol and Ezal Diin Abdallah, we established the office and educated the masses about the vision of New Sudan. Our office conducted many political rallies and activities such as participation in the welcoming of SPLM/A's Chairman to Khartoum, Dr John Garang de Mabior on 8 July 2005, at Green Square.

We also participated extensively in the April 2010 general election campaign, and Cde. James Makur Mading Maker was our candidate for constituency No. (1), Al Kamlen to the National Parliament, Dr. Mohammed Yousif Ahmed Al Mustafa for Gezira State Governorship and Yasir Saeed Arman who was the SPLM's presidential candidate. We did campaign sincerely and were wise of victory before an unfortunate surprise withdrawal from National elections. Through SPLM political organisations, I became a member of SPLM interim Liberation Council of Al Gezira State and later with other comrades elected to represent Al Gezira State in the SPLM Second National Convention in May 2008. We were five Southerners from Al Gezira, Cde Abdallah Abukor, who was the Deputy Chairperson, Hon. Lillian Andrea, an MP in Al-Gezira State's Legislative Council, Cde Ogawe Ojuok, Cde Solomon Ayei, Cde James Makur Mading and myself.

Being an SPLM member at the state level gave me an opportunity to have a clue about CPA's implementation process generally and Abyei Protocol in particular. I continued my activities in SPLM North, Gezira State, until I came to Abyei in June 2010, where I lost heart and ceased political activism. I volunteered in Abyei Secondary School shortly before being contracted by the Carter Center which observed Sudan's elections in April 2010, and again at the referendum of Southern Sudan. I served as an interpreter for Carter Center's Team for Northern Warrap (Twic) and Abyei.

Following the inauspicious deferral of the Abyei referendum, Carter Center was just following the related developments through interviews with politicians, civil societies and traditional leaders. Working with the Carter Center allowed me to have a clear picture of how the Abyei referendum was eluded and its implications especially among Ngok Dinka of Abyei. I had been to many villages in the northern part of Abyei up to Setteb and had visited most of the inhabited hamlets in Abyei Area.

On social respect, I was brought up in a humble family wisely coached by our beloved and caring father whom death had hurriedly snatched from us. Human mortality is a bad reality, though we are all destined for it, and should emotionally be prepared. There was no more heartbreaking moment I ever went through than the inopportune death of my father on 21 April 2001, in Shendi. It was excruciating and I felt so bereft to the extent of shedding no tears for almost a whole week. My father died when I was in Al-Gezira -Bageir Industrial Locality working as a Primary School Teacher in St. Thomas Moore's Combonian School. As a young adult in my early twenties stepping towards manhood, I could have learned much from his insightfulness, nevertheless, I was considered lucky to have spent all my teenage years close to him and fully enjoyed his talents as a great chanter, history teller and a poet.

In the first week after my father's demise, I tried to conceptualise the picture of how life would look without him. It was so much murkier. Father, I am honestly gratified, wherever and whenever your name *Alor Bulabek Biong aka Alor Manyiel* is mentioned among your peer group. It is often received with praise and grace. Carrying your name is inestimable and much worthy than any inherited wealth. I am very proud of you as a son and a protègé.

Abyei - 14 June, 2023

PART 1

THE GENESIS
OF THE ABYEI
POLITICAL QUESTION

"It has been decided that Sultan Rob (Arop) whose country is on the Kiir River, and Sheikh Rihan of Toj (Twic), mentioned in the last intelligence report, are to belong to Kordofan Province. These people have, on certain occasions, complained of raids made on them by Southern Kordofan Arabs, and it has been advisable to place them under the same Governor as the Arabs of whose conduct they complained."

Sudan's Intelligence report
28 March, 1905

CHAPTER 1

A SOLUTION
TURNED INTO A PROBLEM

Abyei is a region of 10,546 square kilometres located between Sudan and South Sudan which was accorded special administrative status by the 2004 Accord (Abyei Protocol). It has pristine agricultural soil, pastures for animals grazing and is rich with natural resources such as oil, gum-producing trees and unmined minerals. This strategic location and richness of resources had invited the political rapacity of others and turned it into a curse. Abyei's issue has stuck not because of political ambiguity, documental inadequacy or legal inapplicability, but Riverine's domineering elites of Sudan, driven by economic rapacity, kept Abyei hostage in the North in order to exploit its resources.

The direct interaction of a political nature between Abyei's traditional leadership and northern authorities is believed to have been some time back during the Mahadia's revolution against the Turks. Chief Arob Biong, identified in British records as Sultan and even as Mek (King), was the first Dinka leader to visit the Muslim revolutionary leader Mohamed Ahmed, known as the Mahdi, the Islamic Messiah. The two established a relationship through which Chief Arob secured Dinka slaves, Southerners that he returned to their respective southern tribes.[1]

However, some sort of intersocietal contact existed between Ngok and some Arab progenies, Al Hamar and Riziegat, before Misseriya arrived in the region of Kordofan. This could be traced through folkloric songs, particularly the poetry of war. Ngok Dinka of Abyei is a sub-section of Padang group in Jieng ethnicity which mostly inhabits the region of Upper Nile. Despite their geographical exposure to the north, Abyei people had courageously and steadfastly managed to safeguard their elements of African cultures, social norms and traditional beliefs. People of Abyei are ethnically and culturally part of the historical and modern fabric of then Southern Sudan region, now the Republic of South Sudan.

Despite the appalling conditions, people of Abyei had existed in the past and shall overcome these temptations of the present, like the political Judas or not. According to folktales and some hodiernal writings, it is widely believed that Ngok people of Abyei came to this present area from Upper Nile in the early seventeenth century when Misseriya were still subjects of Wadai kingdom which is Chad in the present day. Following the collapse of Al-Mahadia, a Pro-Mahadi Dervish by name Ali Julla returned

---

1   *Abyei between the two Sudans*, p12

to Kordofan and distracted the local communities which were living in relative peace. He launched slave trade activities on the neighbouring black communes at the border between the North and South Sudan. As a result, leaders of the victimised communities raised complaints to colonial administration.

Hence, in 1905 the Anglo– Egyptian Condominium Rule transferred Abyei with some other affected areas to Kordofan province from Bahar el Gazal and Upper Nile. This decision was described as prudent and considered to have been the best way to address the challenges. Below is the order of the transfer. [2]

> *It has been decided that Sultan Rob (Arop) whose country is on the Kiir River, and Sheikh Rihan of Toj, mentioned in the last intelligence report, are to belong to Kordofan province. These people have, on certain occasions, complained of raids made on them by southern Kordofan Arabs, and it has been considered advisable to place them under the same Governor as the Arabs of whose conduct they complained.* [3]

This was how the transfer came about; it was merely administrative. Yes, leaders of the said communities complained, but did

---

2   Douglas H Johnson, *The road back from Abyei p2:* Twic was transferred back to Bahar el Ghazal in 1912 and Ruewng to Upper Nile in 1931. See the timetable of the boundaries change 1905-1960 Douglas Johnson *Southern boundaries:* Background Paper Appendix 13

3   Sudan's intelligence report (SIN) 128-1905

not request a transfer, nor any sort of consultation was made to educate the people. Nonetheless, genuine attempts were made to revert Abyei back to South Sudan before colonial administration's departure but collided all with strong convictions of Ngok leadership of the day, Kuol Arop in 1930s and his son Deng Majok in 1950s, who were skeptical and believed that the same factors which caused the transfer still existed. This issue became a matter of division and Ngok community was radically polarised into exponents and opponents.[4]

Relations between Ngok and Misseriya witnessed relative placidity before and during the reign of Paramount Chief Deng Kuol (Deng Majok) who ensured his father Sultan Kuol Arop and Babo Nemir succeeded his father on the other side of Misseriya Ajaaira. The defining factor of that transitory stability was the power equation. Tribesmen of the two notorious communities were using primitive weapons in which Ngok was a little bit superior to Misseriya before the central government intervened by supplying Misseriya with sophisticated weapons.

Tong Ngol (Ngol's fight-1965) was a watershed, turning the relations between Ngok and Misseriya unmendable. Ngol is a seasonal branch of Kiir River running from north-west to the east. Villages of Maper Amaal, Rumthil, Langar, Mabek, Pawol and Dakjur were all located along Ngol river. The incident occurred when Misseriya killed a member of Lou Aguer Geng, a Dinka

---

4   Douglas H Johnson, *Abyei, the CPA and the war in Sudan's new South* p5. Arop Madut, *The Ngok Dinka of Abyei: South Sudan in historical perspective* pp 124–127

subsection in Awiel East which used to seasonally migrate to Abyei to avoid floods of their areas during the rainy seasons. The man was killed in Maper Amaal village, and his arms were amputated and used as sticks for drums. That bestial act had provoked the Ngok Dinka, ergo, they attacked Misseriya. In response, Misseriya came in phalanxes, burned the villages and brutishly killed elderly women and children, but Ngok courageously fought back and repulsed the attacks. This battle is popular among Ngok as Tong-Ngol, the battle of Ngol. It was a significant malefic historical juncture which arguably determined the relation between Ngok and Misseriya.[5]

Ngok elders of different generations kept instilling this particular battle in the minds of their youth. It is said that leaders of the warring tribes, Deng Majok of Ngok Dinka and Babo Nimer of Misseriya AJ'aaira were almost shooting each other, if not for the intervention of the accompanying police. This happened when the two leaders were checking the battle fields and first found a site where Dinka were killed.

Babo did not hide his emotions, and celebratorily declared the victory saying, *The harba* [big spear] *is now proved useful and I will increasingly supply it to my children.*

Deng Majok swallowed the bitter pill. While advancing, they this time reached a site where Misseriya were sadistically killed, Deng Majok reciprocally responded by saying, *It is now proved that Aban-ban* [the kind of spear which Ngok used], *is much useful,*

---

5   Ngok oral history interview with the chiefs Anei Ajak Malual/ Wun Kur and Chok Dengabot Kuol

therefore, I will let it be extra produced to my children. Babo reacted furiously and pointed his gun at Deng Majok who instantaneously did the same.

In retaliation for their losses in Ngol (1965), Misseriya gathered all Dinka who were residing in their main towns of Babanusa and Muglad and burned them alive. It was an unprecedented, heartbreaking crime in the North and South Sudan's history, the estimated number was hundreds of men, women and children. The worst part is that the massacre happened while police forces were indifferently watching that drama of human degradation without intervention. That event taught Ngok a lesson that Sudan's government neither considers them citizens, nor human beings whose lives are valued and deserve protection. If there was an impartial investigation conducted, the government could have been found involved in all phases of that crime from incubation to hatching.

Essentially, it is Government's duty to safeguard people's lives and apply the rule of law on all its citizens irrespective of their race, region, religion, culture or political affiliations. This crime committed against Ngok and other Southerners in Babanusa and Muglad is tantamount to an act of genocide.

In 1970, Moyak Deng ensued his late paramount chief Deng Majok who died in 1969. As a result of the Ngok tendency to protect their guests (southerner fellows) who seasonally come to Abyei area, the government forces assassinated Chief Moyak Deng together with his brothers Chan Deng Kuol, Bulabek Deng Kuol and elders, Thuc Chol Gueiny (Thuc Aliet) and Kiir Jaal. Chief Moyak had reprobated the killing of Southern Sudanese cattle keepers and the confiscation of their properties. SAF envisaged

Moyak as pro Southern Sudan. Arabs don't differentiate between southerners, being just black was more than enough to make one a target. That was how Ngok explicitly understood it, and therefore, decided to fight Misseriya and revenge any killing of a fellow Southerner. Protecting a guest is a common moral ethos in Jieng, an outsider who is officially a guest deserves protection. Jieng people believe it is a curse-causer and despise worthy to allow a guest to be humiliated in your home.

By what was believed to have been an underhanded influence of some of Misseriya's generals in Sudan's Armed Forces, the Government took an outrè decision by forming a paramilitary force to accompany the nomadic Arabs on their seasonal migrations in Kordofan. This decision was overtly said to prevent frictions between cattle keepers and the stable agrarian communities, but appeared later to have been politically motivated. The fact was that nomadic Arabs were armed against Southern Sudanese in general, Ngok and all border tribes in particular. This was subsequently proved from the way forces were selectively recruited, mostly from border tribes of Misseriya and Reziegat. The same chaotic policy was applied later in Darfur by establishing a paramilitary force that favors Arabs against the African ethnicities. But as the aphoristic saying goes, *What goes around, comes around.* This discordant racial stratagem backfired on its ensnarers in Khartoum when the deep State collided furiously with its own made, Janjaweed empire, a situation which embodies the Sudanese epigrammatic saying that *Whoever digs a hole with intentions of trapping others, falls in his own hole.*

Dr. John Garang de Mabior, the founding father and

Commander in Chief of the SPLM/A was one of the Sudanese political mavens who did impeccably expound the Sudanese socio-cultural maladies and accurately diagnose their related political dilemmas. He clearly stated that *the government of the National Islamic Front (NIF) would rather be followed by the New Sudan Government, or Sudan will breakup into many countries.*[6] That was in Chukudom in the SPLM/A's first convention in April 1994, and he repeatedly said it in his historical speech in Nyaio stadium, that *Sudan can't and won't be the same again.* His prognosis came true as Riverine's political elites, despite a clear roadmap drawn in the Comprehensive Peace Agreement to hold Sudan united, insisted on swimming against pluranimity's tide as did their predecessors during the post-colonial era. Instead of accepting the rich socio-cultural, religious and racial diversity as an incentive factor and utilising it for building the Sudanese Nationalism, elites opted to embrace a pseudo identity of 'Islam-Arabisim' which excludes the majority of the Sudanese population, hence resulting into secession of Southern Sudan and the worst is expected to come. [7]

Misseriya committed another wanton crime which was no less brutal than that of Babanusa and Muglad in 1977, and the victims were exclusively from Abyei. This horrid incident took place when Misseriya section of AJ'aaira, which seasonally migrates to Abyei, ambushed many vehicles. Nearly one hundred men, women and children were brutishly killed, among the victims, Mark Mijak

---

6   Dr. John Garang's opening speech in SPLM 1st National Convention/ Chukudom April 1994

7   Dr. John Garang's speech in Nyaio stadium in Kenya 2005

Abiem who was doing his PhD field research and a lecturer in the University of Khartoum. This massacre is one of the gloomiest pages in the history of Ngok and Misseriya, victims were mostly youths. You feel how harrowing it was and still overwhelming whenever re-narrated.[8]

No matter how politics may be considered dynamic, the brutal killing of the renowned academic, Mark Mijak Abiem and Ngok's irreplaceable hero, Kuol Adol Deng Kuol won't go unnoticed, it shall be carried on as an assignment for coming generations. Though it is an unaltered reality that Ngok and Misseriya shall inevitably exist as neighbours, whether in one country or in two separate countries, but it's inconceivable to realise peaceful coexistence before Misseriya relinquishes its crimelike lifestyle.

The painful fact that connected all those inhumane massacres was impunity, Khartoum government held no one accountable, perpetrators were known, but intentionally kept unknown for reasons best known to it. Since Misseriya had the central government at her back and Maraheel paramilitary forces moving with them, the power equation became unbalanced in their favour. Maraheel forces drove Ngok out of their villages through continuous horrid attacks. This diabolical campaign was meant to displace Ngok and replace with Arabs. With SAF help, Ngok's northern villages turned into seasonal residential sites and Misseriya grazing habitats. This was of course a government-supported oblique strategy to displace Ngok from their northern hamlets and squeeze in Abyei Town.

---

8   Chief Anei Ajak Malual, Ngok oral history

In September 1985, Misseriya attacked the village of Dungob Alie, killed more than fifteen and looted all the cattle. That same week, SPLA insurgents captured one of 31st Brigade's sergeants named Mohammed Noor Saeed. He was keeping his goats in the house of a woman called Koom Mammedh. This soldier visits Koom frequently to check his properties, he in exchange supplies her with sugar and salt for keeping his belongings. Mohammed Noor established friendly contacts with Koom and was popularly bynamed as Jur Koom (Koom's Arabic man). On that day when Mohammed Noor was visiting his friend Koom as usual, he met with her (Koom) on the way, but she never informed him about SPLA presence, Mohammed Noor was eventually captured and killed. As result, SAF retaliated and started targeting people accusing them of being SPLA informants. [9]

Many were assassinated including Bulabek Kon Tingloth, Chom Mading, and Lueth Dheil widely known as Matong-goor. When news spread, people were intensely grieved, I remember how Father was saddened upon receiving the news of Lueth Matong-goor's assassination. We were by then in Minyang Anyiel. Koom was later detained by 31st Brigade notorious military intelligence, subjected to inhumane investigation and continued torture, and she died in that detention centre which is now the Ministry of Finance. The torture was assigned to a dedicated killer and a tormentor, Mohammed Mastoor who sometimes used panga in

---

9   Interview with politicians and Civil Societies Activist/ Hon. Deng Kiir Mateir, Hon. Aguer Nyok Bar and Mulana Mayol Deng Dau

cutting people alive. He was cursed by Ngok innocent people's blood whom he unjustly butchered. All his children were said to have been born incomplete. Mohammed Mastoor remained in Abyei until he was killed by a Rocket Propelled Grenade (RPG) near the church residential area (Hai Kanisa) in Abyei during 2008 incidents. With SAF's extravagant brutality, massive killing and re-launching of human raids, Abyei's northern villages were forcefully evacuated.

PART 2

ABYEI: A CASE OF POLITICAL DERELICTION

If martyrs from Abyei who sacrificed their lives for the liberation of South Sudan could resurrect and find out how the issue of their home area is being contemptuously dealt with, they would know their sacrifices were betrayed.

CHAPTER 2

NGOK:
THE GATE GUARDERS

Abyei Area is one of the northernmost Southern Sudan's areas
bordering the north. This geographical location has some
beneficent and malefic effects, it continues to be a central factor
in many ways as far as Abyei's political destiny is concerned. It
also contributed to shaping the collective characteristics of its
inhabitants, whether sophistication, flexibility or resilience for
enduring hardships. As the saying goes, *People are sons of their own
environment*, meaning circumstances play greater roles in shaping
people's traits.

As a matter of fact, if anything disadvantaged the people of
Warrap for instance, Abyei could have double-drank from it first.
This made them more mature in handling countless challenges
which they continuously encountered throughout history. One of

these challenges was the confrontation of slave-trade raids which northern slave traders launched against southern border communities. Southerners at the borderline were vulnerably exposed, hence fell victim, particularly to Kordofan slave traders. Ngok had also, under the leadership of Sultan Arob Biong, managed to prevent what could have imposed imminent threats on Ngok territory and beyond. Following the conquest of Mohammed Ahmed al Mahadi and proclamation of his religious state in Omdurman, the next strategic political move was territorial expansion.

Sultan Arop Biong already knew the potential effect that this new system could thrust on Ngok community, who had just heard the news of the advent of a religious leader (Bany-Bith/Spear Master), but didn't know his exact message. Therefore, Arop and his peers in Ngok leadership decided to draw near instead of waiting.

This move could be considered a show of authority as an independent Sultanate. Arop Biong formed a high delegation from Ngok's spiritual leaders, dignitaries and strong fighters, to mention, Alor Ajiing, the head of Mannyuar Chiefdom and overall Spear Master of Dhendior lineages was a co-leader. Among them also Bulabek Biong Alor (author's grandfather), Mijak Kuoldit Biong Alor and others.

After a long journey on foot (Leaders were on horses) of nearly a month, Arop and his entourage reached Omdurman and were well received.

That outreach policy was very successful, he managed to convince Al-Mahadi to release the southern slaves, and brought them back to be distributed to their respective communities. Through valiant and wise leadership, Arop Biong safeguarded his people and the neighboring communities from a probable aggression.[10]

Abyei's people, like other Southern Sudanese communities at South-North borders, were victims of anti-south policies practised by successive governments since the independence of Sudan. However, Abyei's case was the worst after being subjoined to Kordofan. This geopolitical factor disfavored Ngok community and awakened in them an unflagging desire for returning to their origin.

When Abyei's issue reached a deadlock, the International Crisis Group published a report on Abyei's political situation and the roles played by sons of Abyei in Southern Sudan's Liberation movements. Below is part of the Crisis Group's report on 12 October 2007. Following Sudanese independence in1956, the Dinka and Misseriya have been pulled towards opposite sides of the country's civil wars. The first, from 1956 to1972, polarised the communities along North-South lines. The turning point was 1965 when 72 unarmed Ngok Dinka in the Misseriya town of Babanusa were burned alive by a mob in a police station to which they had fled for protection. The Dinka began to gravitate increasingly towards the southern rebel Anya-Nya and the south's cause, while the Misseriya received preferential treatment from the central government and identified firmly with the North. The 1972 Addis Ababa agreement, which ended the first war, included a clause for a referendum to allow "any other areas that were culturally and geographically part of southern complex", including Abyei, to choose between

---

10   Chief Anei Ajak Wun Kur, Ngok oral history

remaining in the north or joining the new autonomous southern region. The referendum was never held and attacks against
Dinka continued throughout the 1970s, leading to forming a
Ngok Dinka unit of Anya-Nya two in the small southern rebellion
that began in Upper Nile in 1975.[11]

The second Civil War began in June 1983 with the birth of the
SPLA. Many Ngok Dinka joined the Anya-Nya Two from Abyei
played a leading role in the foundation of the new movement.
Displacement of the Ngok Dinka, which had begun during the
first Civil War and continued throughout the 1970s, escalated
during the second war. In part because of their early support, many
from Abyei came to hold senior military and political positions
in the SPLA and had close links with its late Chairman, Dr John
Garang. As the war dragged on, the call for independence grew
stronger among southerners, including the Ngok. However, the
discovery of oil complicated matters in Abyei as in other oil-rich
areas close to the north-south borders. After the initial discovery
in 1979, then president Nimieri attempted—the first of many
efforts—to alter the boundaries and relocate oil-rich areas from
southern to northern Sudan.

The Misseriya joined the war on the Government's side in the
mid-1980s, providing frontline forces against the Dinka in Abyei
and further south in the form of Murahleen, horseback raiders
who attacked southern villages to loot and take slaves as part of
organised offensives against the SPLA and southern civilians. The

---

11   International Crisis Group reports 12 October 2007, briefing
on the deadlock of Abyei issue

July 2002 Machakos Protocol provided the framework from which the CPA grew: in exchange for northern Sudan remaining under Sharia law (Islamic law). The South would get an autonomous government and a self-determination referendum on secession or unity after a six-year interim period. It defined southern Sudan within the borders existing at independence on 1 January 1956, thus excluding Abyei from participation in the self-determination referendum along with northern SPLA strongholds in the Nuba Mountains (Southern Kordofan) and southern Blue Nile (now Blue Nile State).

Abyei's elites understood that their political question was yielded to northerners as a scape goat, therefore, reoriented their people for another cycle of struggles. The Abyei Liberation Front (ALF) was founded in 1978 by Deng Alor, James Ajiing, Arop Madut, Edward Lino and Col. Deng Alek and under the chairmanship of Dr. Zacharia Bol Deng (Arop, 2012). Its main objectives included building a united leadership for Abyei, working towards the holding of a referendum, mobilising funds and resources to buy guns for Abyei's self-defense, and influencing the leadership of the South to support the cause of Abyei. The formation of the ALF proceeded from a meeting of Abyei intellectuals in Juba with Abel Alier, then president of the South, after the devastation of the Abyei area in 1977. At this meeting, he had made it clear that (in his opinion) the issue of Abyei was insoluble and that, if they were not careful, the people of Abyei would end up like the Palestinians; joining Kordofan was preferred to annihilation (Kuol, 2013). According to Arop Madut, a Ngok Dinka journalist and historian, this was why the intellectuals formed the ALF and worked with the 'wind of change' movement to bring down Abel Alier. The ALF set about acquiring arms for the people of Abyei and training them to defend themselves from the Misseriya and Murahleen. In 1981, a group of Ngok Dinka intellectuals and chiefs were having an evening social gathering in Abyei Town when they were attacked by government forces. A primary school teacher was killed, and a number of intellectuals, senior officials and the Ngok paramount chief Kuol Deng fled to the Bahar el Ghazal. After this incident, the Abyei Anya-Nya Two was organised by Miokol Deng, with support from the ALF. He led a force out of Abyei to the Twic area and, together with the Malual Dinka Anya-Nya Two began intensive local training. The forces of Abyei Anya-Nya Two were involved in the attack on Ariath, a station along the railway linking north and south, in early 1983, in an incident that shocked Khartoum.[12]

Miokol was assisted in his work by many students, including Pieng Deng, an engineering student at the University of Khartoum, and by Bagat Agwek, a soldier stationed in Juba who managed to smuggle guns into Abyei. In early 1983, Miokol and Bagat played a significant role in uniting various Anya-Nya Two groups in the Bahar el Ghazal. It has been estimated that Miokol Deng brought some 10,000 fighters to the nascent SPLM/ Sudan People's Liberation Army (SPLA) at its headquarters at Bilpam; many young people from Abyei died on the way.

Dr John Garang, in his address to the people of Abyei in 2004, recognised the important role played by Miokol Deng (Sudan Mirror, 2007). Besides the Anya-Nya Two organised by Miokol in

---

12   *Abyei: Between the Two Sudans*, pp 38–40

Abyei and the Bahar el Ghazal, groups of students and intellectuals from Abyei Area went to Bilpam in early 1982. Kuol Anyel, the son of Anyel Kuol, who had been assassinated by government forces in 1969 in Abyei Town, was among the first group to go. The arrest of Abyei leaders induced even more Abyei students and intellectuals to join the Anya-Nya Two. After the Bor mutiny, that triggered the rebellion in May 1983, students from the University of Khartoum and University of Juba along with some leading Abyei intellectuals in the South and Khartoum went to Ethiopia and joined the SPLA.

Among those Abyei intellectuals were Deng Alor, a diplomat in the Ministry of Foreign Affairs in Khartoum, Chol Deng, a senior official in the southern regional government, and Mading Deng-Abot, a new graduate of Juba University. Following these developments in the Abyei Area and formation of Abyei Anya-Nya Two, the government of Sudan arrested several Abyei intellectuals and senior Ngok officials in the southern regional government in early 1983 (Deng,1995). About fifty Abyei intellectuals, chiefs and leaders, including their leader Dr. Zacharia, were rounded up in Malakal, Wau, Juba, Khartoum and Abyei. A second wave of arrests of Ngok Dinka intellectuals took place in 1984, which encouraged another wave of Abyei citizens to join the SPLA. These and other developments ultimately led to substantial Ngok Dinka participation in the membership of the SPLA.

These facts prove unambiguously that people of Abyei were not adjunct participants in the Liberation of Southern Sudan, but proactive. They were there from the get-go and shall indefatigably continue their search using all possible mechanisms, noncoercive or anything else if needs be. Ngok people of Abyei had been severely subjected to political persecution and systemic forced displacement, therefore, sacrificed their lives for emancipation. People of Abyei did participate equally in the liberation of South Sudan, they should have been therefore considered stakeholders on equal shoulders with the rest of Southerners., Unfortunately, Kiir's Administration dealt with Ngok people of Abyei inappropriately as if they were subjoins or "Hiwis". (Hiwi is a German term for those foreigners who volunteered to assist the Nazis/ mercenaries).

From the outset, Sudan People's Liberation Army was formed through unification of armed groups and Abyei's Anya-Nya Two was one of them. Ngok peoples of Abyei were victims of Nimieri's mis-implementation of the Addis Ababa Agreement. Abyei related provision was not implemented, unlike the other parts of Southern region which relatively enjoyed the fruits of autonomous rule before Addis Ababa Agreement was entirely short-lived.

In any case, the period between Addis Ababa and Machakos is three decades (1972-2002) through which people of Abyei heroically participated in the war and many martyred as Southern Sudanese freedom fighters not Ngok of Kordofan as Bona Malwal Madut and his zany mouthpieces nauseously reprise with impunity. Ngok's initiation of insurgency was a protest against political injustice and selective implementation of the Addis Ababa Agreement. It is therefore unacceptable that their political question regressed after decades of struggle.

If martyrs from Abyei whose blood poured all over Southern Sudan could resurrect, read Machakos Protocol, and see how their homeland had been deprivileged, they would know their sacrifices were squandered in a sinister manner.

CHAPTER 3

ABYEI FROM ADDIS ABABA
TO MACHAKOS (1972–2002)

*Abyei's people did not join Anya-Nya movements and
Sudan People's Liberation Army (SPLA) to be lesser
South Sudanese. Leaving Abyei out of Machakos was
an inexpiable mistake, it marked a beginning of another
history of political dereliction.*

Abyei's question was not politically so equivoque, but intricated
by Khartoum's successive governments. The transfer ordered
by colonial rule was administrative and changed nothing in Ngok's
traditional administration's structure. Despite the fact that the two
communities of Ngok and Misseriya were placed under the British
Administration of Kordofan, they remained separate entities. After
Sudan gained independence, national governments could have

resolved the issue of Abyei by simply re-transferring it to Bahar el Gazal. However, Khartoum's intention on Abyei was precisely disclosed during the Addis Ababa Agreement when the Area was detached from Southern Sudan. Thanks to Dr. Francis who intervened and pushed for the inclusion of Abyei political cause. In an interview on his roles in advancing the cause of Southern Sudan and Abyei in particular, Dr. Francis stated the following:

> *The committee preparing for the talks was meeting. My colleague, Natale Olwak, lecturer in the University of Khartoum, and a member of the committee, invited me to attend the meeting. The specific issue under consideration was the definition of South Sudan. It was agreed that South Sudan comprised of the three provinces of Bahar el Gazal, Equatoria and Upper Nile. I raised my hand and was given the floor. I asked whether they were not leaving out of their definition an area that was part of Southern Sudan.*
>
> *My question was met with laughter as they all understood that I was of course alluding to Abyei, so, the definition was adjusted to include Abyei and other areas that South claimed were wrongly occupied by the north. The Addis Ababa Agreement was of course an endorsement of regional autonomy as a principle of unity in diversity. Abyei proved to be a very divisive issue, as Khartoum insisted that it was part of the North, while the South saw it as part and parcel of the south. In the end, Abel Alier, who led the government delegation,*

negotiated compromise by which Ngok would decide the
status through a plebiscite. [13]

This was how that generation of Southern Sudanese politicians were weak willed on Abyei's political cause. Imagine Southerners alone counterfactually excluding Abyei from the definition of what would legally and politically be a recognised region of Southern Sudan!

When I form, with the mind's eye, a view of the theatre above which was a preparatory meeting for Addis Ababa, compared to what happened in Machakos, I find no difference, only characters, places and times, but political attitude on Abyei remains the same.

Even though Abyei was detached from the autonomous administration in Juba, Dr. Francis Deng managed to convince President Nimeri and secured a diminutive autonomous-like administration for Abyei under the Presidency.

It is often said that *Wrong beginnings lead to wrong conclusions.* This issue of Abyei had been already betrayed from the beginning when parties were negotiating the General Principles (GPs) in Machakos. Abyei, together with Nuba Mountains and South Blue Nile were elided from the main negotiation's platform of IGAD.

When the terms of the Machakos Protocol were made
public, there was a near revolt within the SPLA. Not

---

13   *Contributions of Dr. Francis Deng to South Sudan and Abyei* Part 3, published in *City Review* newspaper, Juba. Interviewed by Mawien Deng Kuol, United States 2022

only were there senior figures from Abyei within the movement who were close to Garang, but there were some 10,000 Nuba SPLA stationed in the South whose loyalty and support were critical to the war effort there. Garang had to support Salva Kiir Mayardit, the SPLM's chief negotiator at Machakos, but he also had to press for the inclusion of issues of Abyei, the Nuba mountains, and Blue Nile in the main negotiations, against Khartoum resistance. In the end, Khartoum would agree only to separate negotiations over the three areas outside main IGAD talks, under Kenyan chairmanship. Since Kenya appointed the IGAD mediator General Sumbeiywo as chair of the Three Area talks the separation from the IGAD negotiations appeared cosmetic, but their separation from negotiations was to have a negative impact on the outcome.[14]

Reading Johnson's statements above, Garang had to support Salva Kiir Mayardit, but he also had to press for the inclusions of issues of Abyei, the Nuba Mountains, and Blue Nile. One could sniff out the fact that SPLM leadership was not on the same page in regard to Abyei SPLM negotiants in Machakos focused prejudicially on the cause of Southern Sudan. Despite their leading roles in the SPLM/A, the Abyei leader's influence was inconspicuous in Machakos, simply because it was about Southern Sudan and

---

14   Douglas H Johnson/ *Abyei, the CPA and the war in Sudan's new South* p13

Abyei was not considered as part of it. This is a bitter truth and has to be expressed without pretext. After managing to alienate Abyei from IGAD main forum where Southern Sudan's issues were being discussed, the National Congress Party insisted to deny Abyei the right to self-determination.

In its report on the Abyei deadlock, the Crisis Group mentioned the following:

> *The Three Areas, and Abyei in particular, were one of the most difficult issues throughout the CPA negotiations. The main disagreement was whether Abyei would be granted a referendum with an option to join Southern Sudan, which implied the possibility of joining an independent South after the southern self-determination referendum in 2011. This was a core SPLM demand. With senior representation from Abyei in the movement leadership, Garang had little flexibility. The government consistently refused to consider a referendum for Abyei (arguing that the Machakos Protocol had already closed that door, and Abyei must remain in the north).*[15]

Reading the last two lines above together with Dr. Johnson's statement, one could incontestably conclude that carving Abyei out of Machakos framework predetermined its fate. The way Abyei was jettisoned in Machakos makes it very hard to resist the surmise that Ngok Dinka's longstanding political foe had used

---

15   Crisis Group 12 October 2007

his intimate relationship with the Chief Negotiator for influencing SPLM's position. One full year after Machakos was signed (July 20th 2002–June 2003), Sudan People's Liberation Movement organised a conference for the people of Abyei in Agok Area, where some radicalists from Twic of Warrap claim now as their territory. Most of SPLM/A senior leaders attended, Dr. John Garang, Salva Kiir, Dr. Riak Machar, Kuol Manyang, Pagan Amum and others.

Nonetheless, the timing of the Agok conference was noticeably irrelevant to its aspired objectives. If this conference was really meant to have an impact on negotiations, it should have been conducted before the peace talks. Below are some of Agok Conference's main resolutions:

a. Ngok Dinka declared unequivocally that the Area is part and parcel of Southern Sudan;

b. Fully mandate the SPLM as the legitimate representative of the Abyei cause in all national, regional and international forums.

These resolutions could have been of great value, if they had been structurally made part of SPLM negotiation's position in Machakos. However, political critics believe Agok Conference was just a perfunctory move "pro forma" to diminish the noticeable disgruntlement of the people of Abyei.

Talks deadlocked on Abyei and that raised the international community's concerns, hence, some hasty moves followed to save the peace from collapsing. United States sent senator John Danforth who extensively engaged the parties and managed to narrow the gap. As result, a convoluted proposal was tabled on 19 April 2003 which represents the US stand as an instrument to break through the stalemate. Danforth did it in a complex manner to balance between parties' positions. On 26 May 2008, a protocol was signed between the Government of Sudan and Sudan People's Liberation Movement/Army (SPLM/A) on the resolution of Abyei conflict. Here are some of the guidelines:

1.1.1 Abyei is a bridge between the north and the south, in linking the people of Sudan;

1.1.2 The territory is defined as the area of the nine Ngok Dinka Chiefdoms transferred to Kordofan in 1905;

1.1.3 The Misseriya and other nomadic peoples retain their traditional rights to graze cattle and move across the territory of Abyei;

1.2 Interim period: Upon signing the peace agreement, Abyei will be accorded special administrative status, in which:

1.2.1 Residents of Abyei will be citizens of both Western Kordofan and Bahar el Ghazal, with representation in the legislatures of both states;

1.3 End of Interim period: Simultaneously with the referendum for Southern Sudan, the residents of Abyei will cast a separate ballot. The proposition voted on in the separate ballot will present the following choices, irrespective of the results of the southern referendum:

a. That Abyei retain its special administrative status in the north.

b. That Abyei be part of Bahar el Ghazal.

1.4 January 1, 1956 line between north and south will be inviolate, except as agreed above.

1.5 The residents of Abyei shall be:

a. Members of Ngok Dinka community and other Sudanese residing in the area.

b. The criteria of residence shall be worked out by the Abyei referendum commission.[16]

Reading the provisions of the Abyei Protocol, particularly articles (1.1.1, 1.2.1, 1.4. a, b), you would understand that mediators were less concerned of future uncertainties that may occur due to self-interested eisegesis of the vague provisions (partisan interpretations). They were obsessed with achieving a crude peace, forgetting that the devil often appears in the details. The Government of Sudan and the Sudan People's Liberation Movement signed the Abyei Protocol, but each kept in mind biases regarding the contentious articles.

The agreement on Abyei was in fact a deferment of the conflict, not a resolution. However, no one had believed that NCP's government would be cooperative. Nonetheless, hope was big on the international community's will in bringing peace to the impaired people of Sudan who have for decades been subject to inhuman sufferings.

Given the degree of mistrust between Northern and Southern Sudan, many South Sudanese were relying on SPLA. Thanks to Dr. John Garang, who shrewdly kept SPLA separate, a matter he criticised in Addis Ababa security arrangements. The formation of Abyei Boundaries Commission was one of the key provisions tactically used by NCP for cunctation. According to the Abyei Protocol, ABC's mandate was to determine and delineate the boundary of Ngok Dinka's territory, which was transferred to

16   Abyei Protocol

Kordofan in 1905, and report to the presidency. Parties disagreed in the interpretation of most provisions such as the boundaries, residents of Abyei and security arrangements. However, mediators had to find a way to unlock the impasse. US mediators proposed some amendments in fundamental aspects relating to ABC establishment. Hence, Abyei Boundaries Commission was formed as follows:

- Five members representing the Government of Sudan and Misseriya led by Al Drdiri Mohammed Ahmed;
- Five members representing the SPLM/A and Ngok led by Deng Alor Kuol;
- And five experts nominated by IGAD as follows
  ◊ US Ambassador to Sudan Donald Peterson
  ◊ Prof. Douglas H. Johnson representing the United Kingdom
  ◊ another three experts from Kenya, Ethiopia and South Africa.

CHAPTER 4

KHARTOUM'S
DEVIATIONAL STRATAGEM

Experts' Committee did their work and reported it in July 2005. The report was instantaneously rejected by NCP and Misseriya claiming that the committee had exceeded its mandate. This marked the first serious violation made to hinder the implementation of the Abyei Protocol. Interestingly, it was the same month that Dr. Garang was killed in a helicopter crash. Dr. John Garang de Mabior was aware of NCP's nuts and bolts and could have politically confronted those maneuvering tendencies. As 1st Vice President, Chairman of the SPLM and Commander in Chief of the SPLA, he could have functioned his powers to the fullest and used other potential political cards to pressure both NCP and Misseriya. For instance, CPA defines any force other than SAF, SPLA and JIU as illegal and therefore considered a militia. So the

Popular Defense Force (D'iffa Al Shaabi) which was primarily formed out of tribes of Kordofan and Darfur belt was a militia according to CPA.

National Congress Party's instrumentation of PDF to hinder the implementation of Abyei protocol was a clear violation which should have been institutionally withstood using JIU forces or even SPLA. Regrettably, SPLM was orphaned with the calamitous death of its charismatic leader, Dr. John Garang de Mabior who understood the Riverine Elites' mentality and knew when and how to politically bite back. He anticipated those ill-tendencies, therefore, insisted to keep his forces (SPLA) separate in the security arrangements. However, nothing was more politically scathing to SPLM than Kiir's Leadership self-defeating approach. On the contrary, NCP took a regnant stand, thus, Abyei Protocol was politically frozen.

Many took Dr. Nafi Ali Nafi's gaffe for granted when he portentously uttered that *Abyei political matter is in a refrigerator*[17]. Abyei leaders of the SPLM gave no heed to Nafi's ominous statement. National Congress Party's message was discernible. Abyei Protocol was not meant for implementation. NCP knew that SPLM leadership would not risk the CPA, particularly the Southern Sudan referendum because of Abyei. With that clear knowledge of SPLM's stand, NCP succeeded in renegotiating and tactically forcing amendments on Abyei Protocol.

With Abyei, history insists on repeating itself. This was the same condition during Addis Ababa Agreement when Abyei's related

---

17   Statement attributed to Dr. Nafi Ali Nafi, one of the hawks of the National Islamic Front (NIF)

provision was ignored by President Jaff'ar Mohammed Nimieri and Alier's autonomous administration in Juba was reluctant and did not want to lose its cordial relations with Khartoum. This is a painful fact, but ordinary people have to understand, despite the bewildered role played by Ngok leaders in this regard. Instead of facing the situation realistically, Abyei leaders of the SPLM were so obsequious to their system, hence chose to politically dupe their own people to avoid any possible reaction.

National Congress Party and Misseriya rejected the ABC's report, hence no progress was made. On the ground, tension was escalating and both sides were ferocious following the juncture Abyei's political case was heading to. Heretofore, Ngok people were still having hope on SPLM leadership, unlike Misseriya who began to realise the fact that NCP's focus was only on economic gains (oil fields), contrary to theirs which is water and pastures for their animals.

For National Congress Party, Abyei was strategic, resources and geographical location made it one of the national security's concerns. Furthermore, northerners were anticipating the results of the Southern Sudan referendum, with all signals indicating that it would break away. NCP's strategy was concentrated on perpetuating instability in the area in order to put Abyei Protocol on-hold. As a result, Joint Integrated Units (JIUs) in Abyei became radically polarised due to political tensions between the two parties. Thereafter, clashes erupted in May 14, 2008, an estimated more than 60,000 people fleeing from their homes crossing Kiir River, and many houses were destroyed.

NCP launched tactical attacks on Abyei while SPLM leadership in Juba was preparing for the Second National Convention, a practice then considered the toughest political and organisational test. Since the movement lost its charismatic leader Dr. John Garang de Mabior, numerous challenges within SPLM began to surface uncontrollably. Some senior leaders openly disclosed their unbridled aspiration for leadership; and integration of Southern militants affiliated to central government in Khartoum was not fully achieved. In the meantime, NCP's agents together with some Southern Sudanese political quislings were furtively rumormongering in order to widen the gap between Salva Kiir and what was deviously termed as Garang's Boys.[18]

Before the kick-off of the convention, disagreements transpired during the re-drafting of the basic document: the Vision, Manifesto and Internal regulations. Some internal lobbies suggested that deputies of SPLM's chairman be reduced to one instead of three as in the previous structure. The position of General Secretary was also a big divisive matter. These issues and others heated the political climate in Juba. Thank God, that problematic issue of hierarchy was resolved to remain unaltered after conventioneers were consulted in their separate groups. It was also believed that the presence of SPLM's old friend, late Roger Winter and South Sudanese eminent personalities, namely, Mulana Abel Alier Kwai and Gen. Joseph Lago Yanga might have played a greater role in unlocking the stalemate.

SPLM Second National Convention's motto was,

"*No for War, Yes for New Sudan.*"

---

18   Author's personal memoir- A member of SPLM Second National Convention from Al Gezira State

The same week, the Justice and Equality Movement (JEM) led by Dr. Khalil Ibrahim attacked Omdurman while Omar Al Bashir was outside the country. Therefore, the convention's preparations were halted and Salva Kiir rushed to Khartoum to handle the situation in his capacity as First Vice President of the Republic of Sudan. When things quietened in Khartoum, Kiir returned to Juba and officially opened the Convention. Concurrently, SAF together with its militias of Popular Defense Forces (PDF) attacked Abyei on 14 May 2008. Surprisingly, the SPLM convention continued normally with the same motto of *No for war, Yes for New Sudan.* That political indifference provoked me while addressing the convention_ I angrily chanted *No peace without Abyei.* However, President Kiir's hasty and impetuous response was so dispiriting, I was later nicknamed by Cde Abdallah Abukor as *a man scolded by the president.*

Unexpectedly, the Abyei delegation gave way to that act of political inconsideration without proper dissent. Abyei Area's delegates were supposed to withdraw to show solidarity with their cause. You cannot stay in a conference whose slogan is No for War, while your own home is being seared! Only Edward Lino then the Administrator for Abyei Area and Dr. Luka Biong accompanied by Roger Winter left the convention and went down to take care of the needy IDPs.

Thereafter, I disbelieved the quixotic conviction that considers SPLM as the only political saviour and started to receive whatever comes from SPLM with a grain of salt.

National Congress Party was on the right track according to its strategy of deviating Abyei Protocol through entangling cycles of political disagreements, followed by insecurity and ending it with new manipulative agreements that derail the Protocol from its legal context. After 2008 truculent incidents in Abyei, National Congress Party and Sudan People's Liberation Movement met to address the new imposed malevolent realities and signed an agreement called Abyei Roadmap in which they agreed on a range of security and administrative issues, such as replacement of units which were involved in the incidents; deployment of police forces through consultation between the National Ministry of Interior and the Ministry for Internal Affairs of the Government of Southern Sudan; appointment of executive administration by the presidency; and the parties also agreed to refer their disagreement on ABC's report to Permanent Court of Arbitration (PCA) in The Hague to determine whether the ABC exceeded its mandate or not. Of course, this was NCP's political intent which I termed as *deviational stratagem*.[19]

According to Abyei Protocol, ABC's report is binding on parties and final. The Annex to the Abyei Protocol and the Rules of Procedure adopted by the Abyei Boundaries commission (ABC) state, in essence, that if the fifteen-person ABC is unable to reach a consensual decision on what the Abyei boundaries should be, the ABC experts' decision shall be final and binding on the parties. Also as noted in the Preface, the Abyei Area has been defined as the area of the nine Ngok Dinka Chiefdoms transferred from Bahar el Ghazal to Kordofan in 1905 (Appendix 1).[20]

As it happened, the two sides, i.e., the Government of Sudan

---

19   Author's personal memoir- A member of SPLM Second National Convention from Al Gezira State

20   Abyei boundaries commission summary report

(GoS) and the Sudan People's Liberation Movement/Army (SPLM/A), were unable to reconcile their differences on the Abyei issue. Thus, the decision arrived at by the five ABC experts was the determinant of the boundaries in question. The experts were:

1. Ambassador Donald Peterson, the Chairman/USA appointee
2. Professor Godfrey Muriuki/ IGAD appointee
3. Professor Kassahun Berhanu / IGAD appointee
4. Dr. Douglas. H. Johnson/ UK appointee
5. Professor Shadrack. B.O. Gutto / IGAD appointee.

SPLM's leadership had made a gross mistake when it knuckled under to NCP's political pressure and went to The Hague. That was a direct concession and renegotiation of CPA and Abyei Protocol in particular.

> *You know, when the issue of Abyei was discussed and resolved in Kenya [in the CPA negotiations], we thought that was it. And we later formed a committee, the Abyei Boundaries Committee, to define the boundaries of the area. The Protocol says the decision of the experts shall be final and binding. When the experts came up with their decision and presented it in July 2005, President Bashir rejected the decision by the experts. That was the first violation of the Comprehensive Peace Agreement. Later, in 2008, they attacked the area, destroyed, burned the town of Abyei. As a result, SPLM and the National Congress went into a very long discussion. At the end, the National Congress suggested that the Dinka were given*

a bigger area, more land than they really deserved, and they said we had to go for international arbitration. The SPLM accepted to go for international arbitration. We went to The Hague; we spent almost one year. And in the end, the ruling that the tribunal came up with, both of us accepted. The ruling was supposed to be, again, final and binding on the parties. Both of us celebrated, and we were going back home. Three or four months later the National Congress started to renege on The Hague ruling. This is where we are now. Now they are coming again and saying, You have to give us the northern part of Abyei We lost almost sixteen thousand square kilometers as the result of The Hague ruling. Now they want us to give them, again, something like four square kilometres.[21]

The tribunal result was pronounced on 22 July 2009. It was unfortunately unfair as some parts of Ngok's native areas were reduced. Court procedure was politically guided, hence focused on making a decision that would be accepted by the Government of Sudan, hence gave priority to Sudan's interest which was oil. As result, vast areas from the north and east were detached, but from the south nothing was changed, and it remained inviolate according to article (1.4) of the Abyei Protocol. The Government of Sudan and SPLM accepted the Arbitration, but Misseriya announced publicly its rejection and readiness to hinder any

---

21   Interview with Deng Alor 29 December 2010 http://allafrica.com

attempt at its implementation. Of course, National Congress Party exploited the Misseriya's ignorance-driven pugnacity and used it as a political tool.

Mostly, Misseriya as a concerned community, was not properly involved in the decision-making mechanisms, as the SPLM was with Ngok, particularly after South Sudan's independence. The only difference was that Ngok had politically authorised SPLM in June 2003, to negotiate on its behalf. This authorisation was still affecting Abyei's issue, particularly when SPLM's leadership of the day decided to use Abyei for its best interests with Khartoum. Misseriya's disregard of the PCA's tribunal amounts to a political "apostasy" which was supposed to have been strongly confronted.

In a conference held in the town of Seteeb, Misseriya threatened to attack any team that would dare to delineate the boundary according to PCA ruling. That was Government's (GoS) position camouflaged by using Misseriya. The Government of Southern Sudan and SPLM on the other side were passive and failed to encounter that serious violation on Abyei Protocol. Henceforth, National Congress Party was able to differentiate between SPLM's strategic and tactical agendas.

SPLM Leadership's irresolute stand on Abyei was subsequently unveiled when National Congress Party attempted to extend Southern Sudan's referendum. Hawks of the Movement turned furious, Pagan Amum Okec, then the Secretary-General, threatened that SPLM/A shall immediately go back to square one (war).

The message was well captured by NCP that Southern Sudan's referendum is a red line. Meanwhile, a large number of ordinary people in Abyei were too dispirited seeing their political destiny being contemptuously dealt with, but despairingly continued to eye the SPLM leadership. Khartoum had pushed Abyei's issue towards its best political interests, however, rejection of PCA and failing to draw the boundaries constituted the major hindrances for Abyei Protocol.

Instead of resolving this fundamental obstacle, SPLM loosely accepted to be dragged on. Despite the fact it was a secret of Polichinelle, that National Congress Party decided to implement the agreement selectively. Ngok leaders of the SPLM ineffectually and biddably played a secondary role in the cause of their own people's political destiny. Parties jumped to enactment of the referendum laws including that of Abyei which was agreed to be concurrently conducted with the referendum of Southern Sudan. Unfortunately, that law was imprecise on the issue of voters' eligibility.

As mentioned earlier, article (1.4 a & b) of Abyei Protocol was a hidden poison in the honey. Instead of addressing the question of voters' eligibility in the law, NCP ill- purposely pushed it to be tackled by a not -yet -formed Abyei's referendum commission.

CHAPTER 5

ABYEI'S INVASION
(19–20 MAY 2011)

While Sudan People's Liberation Movement was engaged solely in the preparations for the referendum of Southern Sudan, National Congress Party inversely managed to set new impediments which deflected Abyei Protocol away from the CPA's main track. Instead of resolving it as an internal question in one Sudan, NCP wanted Abyei to be a disputed region between a sooner-would-be-two sovereign independent States.

In continuity to its divertive strategy, National Congress Party used its armed wings, SAF and Misseriya's militias and launched serial offenses on Abyei to shackle any possibility of conducting the referendum.

"Fighting broke out in and around the Abyei area as voting in the Southern referendum began. No official details have been released yet, but unofficial UN statements report attacks on SPLA police posts by Misseriya gunmen on motorcycles and exchanges of heavy weapons fire elsewhere." [22]

I bore witness to most events of the years 2010–2011 in Abyei. When the north confirmed that Southern Sudan would ineluctably break away it trumped up a propaganda that Abyei's issue may rescind the referendum of Southern Sudan. This political snare was myopically swallowed by some elements and created a wave of antipathy toward the Abyei issue to a degree of phobia, particularly with those perfidious chancers who know little about Abyei's question and form their perceptions base on political scuttlebutts.

On the other hand, Abyei people in the north were excited and much interested in repatriation to ensure effective participation in their referendum. I returned to Abyei with my family in 2010 for the same objective. Abyei Town was overpeopled, though many proceeded to their native villages such as Kolom, Maker, Noong, Midrook, Kol-Bol Agany-tok, Nyien-coor, Todac, Dokura, Amiet, Tajalei, Miokol-Alie, Lau, Ganga, Abathok, Mijak-Manyuar, Mabok, Rumamer, Marial-Acak in the far east, Agok and Miyom Dau Mijok in the far south-east.

Southern Kiir areas had no security challenges except issues to do with adaptation to new environments and building inns.

---

22   Douglas H Johnson/ *The road back from Abyei*, 14 January 2011

Despite the fact that many children and young adults were born in exile (Northern Sudan), all had hastily and energetically managed to eke out their living. Khartoum was closely following all the political developments and continued proxy policy using Misseriya to encumber repatriation. From here, people were exposed to imminent threats on the route, especially in western Kordofan territory. Despite the intervention from the national government which provided protection for convoys, some calamitous incidents were registered.

In his book, *Creating facts on the ground: Conflict dynamics in Abyei* Dr. Joshua Craze had documented all the fatal events committed by NCP and its allies, militants of Misseriya in Abyei, prior to the referendum. To ascertain the abrogation of Abyei referendum, Khartoum tactically launched a series of offenses in most of the northern villages of Abyei Area.

February and March 2011 saw the worst violence in Abyei since 2008, as 154 people died during clashes, mainly between Misseriya militants and Abyei police forces, in the villages of Todac, Tajalei, Maker, Wungok and Dungop which left the first four of these villages partially or totally burned down.[23]

National Congress Party's motive was to invade Abyei and create a de facto situation prior to the independence of Southern Sudan. This was unfortunately realised when SAF, Misseriya and some Southern Sudanese militias (Mercenarian Insurgents of the warlord Abdel-Bagi Ayei Akol) affiliated to Khartoum heavily attacked

---

23   Dr. Joshua Craze, *Creating Facts on the Ground: Conflict dynamics in Abyei*, p34

Abyei on 19–20 May 2011. This ferocious invasion consequently led to forceful mass displacement of population, complete looting and destruction of invaluable keepsakes and properties.

One month after SAF invaded Abyei, the Government of Sudan (GoS) and Sudan People's Liberation Movement (SPLM) signed an agreement called Temporary Arrangements for the Administration and Security of Abyei Area. This move was widely envisaged as a continuation of the same manipulative tactics. SPLM was again trapped into by signing another defective and unrefined deal that utterly serves Khartoum's delay strategy. However, it was undeniable that redeployment of forces, SAF and SPLA out of Abyei Town and their replacement with United Nations Interim Forces for Abyei (UNISAF) helped in revamping relative security in Abyei and allowed the people to gradually return to their respective villages. But politically, it elongated the path to the final status.

Parties to Comprehensive Peace Agreement had unswervingly maintained their stands on Abyei. National Congress Party used Abyei as a potential excuse to incline its obligations in the CPA, while Sudan People's Liberation Movement continued in compromising it to safeguard its ultimate objective, an amicable breakaway of southern region from the north. That's how Abyei Protocol was estranged, any impartial analysis could simply lead to this end.

Describing the political equation between National Congress Party and Sudan People's Liberation Movement on Abyei, Dr. Joshua Craze alluded that NCP was dictating the rules of the game:

"The invasion was also another chapter in the NCP's use of violence as a tool of political negotiation. On

25 May the NCP announced that SAF will only leave Abyei when there is a political settlement (VoA, 2011). Ultimately, this makes SAF the final arbiter in Abyei and a SAF withdrawal now appears as something that the SPLM will have to make concession to achieve.[24]

SPLM Leadership's position was apparent, Abyei was surrendered to the North, but Ngok leaders misthought that the independence of Southern Sudan would ease the resolution of Abyei's final status, something which would subsequently be proved a mere misreading and political myopia.

In his capacity as SPLM chairman in Abyei, Chief Administrator, Lt. Gen. Kuol Diem Kuol once described the demand for autonomous rule for Abyei as infringement of Abyei Protocol and tampering with what he termed as an achieved political status. He further added that people of Abyei were only accorded two options in Abyei Protocol and there is no room for any third option. Gen. Kuol asked about martyrs who might have sacrificed for this political demand.[25] This, in my opinion, was a surreptitious attempt at monopolising the struggle, forgetting that Ngok had offered hundreds of martyrs in self-defense before the advent of his political organisation (SPLM/A). Kuol seemed oblivious that his party had been weak-kneed in accepting many alterations on Abyei protocol throughout the CPA's implementation process. The first

24   Dr. Craze, *Creating Facts*, p43

25   Statement attributed to Lt. Gen. Kuol Diem Kuol in one of SPLM's rallies in Abyei/ August 2022

ever distraction was Abyei roadmap agreement in 2008, Kadogli Agreement on 17 January 2010, and 20 June 2011 Agreement. This renegotiation and reproduction of agreements happened due to SPLM'S sinuous position on Abyei.

Article (2) of the Agreement on Temporary Arrangements for the Administration of Abyei Area reads as follows:

The provisions of this agreement shall not prejudge the final status of Abyei Area whose borders have been defined by the permanent Court of Arbitration. Except as modified by the terms herein, this agreement respects the provisions of the Protocol on the resolutions of Abyei conflict (the Abyei Protocol). The 1 January 1956 line between the North and South will remain inviolate, unless changed as a result of the outcome of the foreseen referendum in the Abyei Protocol or "other decision of the parties on the final status of Abyei.[26]

In the last two lines of the above article, there is a reference to another alternative [or other decision of the Parties on the final status of Abyei] which isn't in Abyei Protocol and may invite interpretational dissension. National Congress Party had politically vanquished the SPLM using its sophistication and diplomatic cognizance, hence managed to hold the Abyei Protocol and strand it at June Agreement's shore. This 20 June egregious deal became a prerequisite for any revival attempt at implementation of Abyei Protocol. (Check the outcome of the summit between heads of state, Omar el Bashir of Sudan and Kiir of South Sudan on 4-5 January 2013 in Addis Ababa. The two presidents

26   The Agreement for Temporary Administrative and Security Arrangements /June 20, 2011/ Addis Ababa

agreed to reconvene on Abyei only after establishment of Joint Administration)

Now people can judge between an imprecise phrase of "other option" in June Agreement which implies double entendre, and a monosemous term of self-rule. SPLM negotiants should have become circumspect, proleptic and more precautional in choosing the terms. They didn't, unfortunately, learn from that confusion created when gullibly accepting the nonspecific phrasing of "other Sudanese" in Abyei Protocol.

Looking at circumstances and apparent exigency for signing the treaty, there is no other interpretation than that the June Agreement was nothing but a "quid pro quo" to protect the independence of Southern Sudan which was in the offing.

PART 3

THE PERTURBATION

It is noble to fight, or even die for freedom of your beloved people, but as humans, you cannot blithesomely celebrate the struggle for freedom that never sets you free. For the people of Abyei region, the struggle continues.

CHAPTER 6

THE FAKE HOPE

When Juba sent delegations to Abyei during the registration for the referendum on self-determination of Southern Sudan, the message was precise. It was clearly conveyed that President Kiir requested from his people of Abyei to allow the dream of all South Sudanese be achieved. Kiir promised that Abyei shall be a priority to a sooner-would-be independent South Sudan. There was no doubt that Abyei sons in SPLM/A leadership were part of that compromise which they might have misconceived as a continuation of Ngok sacrifices for the cause of Southern Sudan. Ngok leaders of the SPLM failed to accurately read those changes which occurred in SPLM sovereign structures.

Following the mistimed death of Dr. John Garang de Mabior, his successor came up with different political convictions and hastily formed new interior and exterior allies which became his exclusive clique. Of course, Salva Kiir Mayardit did not genuinely rub elbows with Abyei's leaders. That geography of affiliation was not a surprise, it could be traced back to the period when leaders from Abyei were in the closed coterie of the former Commander in Chief of SPLM/A Dr. John Garang de Mabior.

Kiir's rift with his boss was an open secret, it surfaced several times but overcame wisely. This contrariness between the two big men of SPLM/A was believed to have been guilefully stimulated by exterior actors who wished to deviate the movement away from its well-thought-out political mission. Among the extraneous elements was Bona Malwal Madut, who was openly averse to the vision of New Sudan, an ideology meant for restructuring the political creed of governance in Sudan. The chief objective of the New Sudan vision was to accommodate the Sudanese diversity. If adopted, it could have been the best political option for governing a multi-ethnic, religious and sociocultural Republic of Sudan. Malwal's opposition could not have been of great effect because he was not a member of SPLM, but he unsavorily meddled in SPLM's internal affairs using his Gogrial Area's Cater Cousins, the likes of late Justin Yac Madut and Salva Kiir Mayardit. Bona was believed to have been the orchestrator and mastermind of Bahar el Ghazal mis-oriented group within SPLM/A. This grouping tendency was in fact a real threat to cohesion of Jieng and SPLM during Liberation time and after. The recalcitrant attitude and contumacious altercation which occurred in Torit Camp (2004) between Dr. John Garang and his deputy Salva Kiir Mayardit was entangled at a critical time as singing of final agreement between the Government of Sudan and Sudan people's Liberation Movement was impending.

The first split of 1991 led by Dr. Riek Machar Teny, Dr. Lam Akol and Gordon Kong was envisaged as a challenge to Dinka leadership, but all were from the same region (Upper Nile), therefore, ethnicity was the effective tool. This time, the case differed, rivals hailed from the same Jieng ethnicity of Bor in Upper Nile and Rek in Bahar el Ghazal, ergo, ethnicity was not fit for purpose, but provincialism and subsectionalism. All divide and rule attempts to fracture and debilitate the movement were believed to have been ensnared by Khartoum. However, instruments used were often Janus-faced southern politicians. When tension intensified between Kiir who was in Yei and Garang in Rumbek, Khartoum's authorities were ebulliently following on a daily basis and that insinuates a probable involvement of Sudan's counterintelligence. In fact, Bona's aversion to SPLM's political project (New Sudan), and his deprecation of Dr. John Garang's character was not an unnoticed matter as alluded to in the statement below.

"During the burial of Dr. John Garang de Mabior in Juba, I saw a contemptuous elder striding toward the graveside at the time when people began to disperse after the burial. The elder was smiling and laughing as he was approaching the grave, flanked by a guy who appeared to be feeling lucky for walking an uncle! That elder was relaxed, walking like he was about to watch a grand football match! None paid him attention because he went un-noticed, casually dressed in sneakers, jeans and a T-shirt. He stood for moments, gazed and left. Neither grief nor a dot of sorrow on his smooth relaxed face, as he

*left the graveside! That elder appeared to have gone there
to make sure that it was Dr. John Garang de Mabior
himself who was buried, the way he appeared. That was
how Malual Madut appeared. Like when he appeared
happy in Juba a day after the attack on Vice-President
Riek Machar's residence on 16th December 2013. Bona
was extremely relaxed when he arrived and Juba was in
turmoil, coming from Khartoum in a Sudan Airways
Boeing 707 on which he was the only passenger!"* [27]

Bona Malwal Madut, a founding member of the Southern
Front Party which emerged in the midst of the 1960s and served
as its first General Secretary, had been sanctimoniously blowing his
own trumpet. He laudatorily alluded in his writings that his party
(SF) was the first political forum which formalised self-determination as a political demand for the people of Southern Sudan. While
this could narrowly be considered, Bona's party had no explicit
instrument for achieving that said self-determination. It therefore,
remained for decades a mere political fantasy, not knowing how
to materialise it. Malwal Madut who was older than Dr. John
Garang and well known in the Sudanese political arena, instead of
joining hands with young John, or autonomously use his colossal
expertise in a constructive manner to achieve whatever he believed
as the right thing for the people of Southern Sudan, chose to
be an underminer and wanted to parasitically claim the credit.
Bona's party was an elite's forum which aimed at power sharing.

---

27   Edward Lino Abyei, *A man to know* pp36-37

SF did not effectuate political awareness amongst the populace in Southern Sudan as later did the SPLM whose political speech motivated the people to step-up for the liberation.

Back to the issue of Abyei, Ngok leaders of the SPLM believed they would manage to reanimate Abyei's file after Southern Sudan's independence, not knowing that Bona Malwal Madut had re-encoded the whole thing leaving those who used to be gurus with no actual access.

Abyei border demarcation, division of national assets, national debt and oil production were the most contentious outstanding issues pushed to be tackled after the independence. Unfortunately, parties to the Comprehensive Peace Agreement, now independent countries, continued their competitive attitude rather than cooperate, hence impeding the implementation of the pending issues. On the other hand, Malwal Madut took it upon himself to undermine the cause of Abyei using whatever mechanisms to achieve his gross intent for seeing Abyei estranged and left for Sudan. To realise his goal, Malwal Madut inculcated into Kiir and Omar Al Bashir's minds, a concept that sons of Abyei and former Garang's inner-circle associates were perilous to peaceful coexistence between Sudan and South Sudan. Thus, he managed through sophistry to utterly inveigle President Kiir to his side, controlled the State's decision and therefore, reaped what he had never sown. After distancing the old crew from decision-making circles, Bona Malwal Madut archived Abyei's file, typified as vexatious and a source of insecurity to South Sudan.

Less than a year after independence of South Sudan, conflict erupted over the oil area of Panthau. Though Khartoum officially accepted the secession, resentment of losing revenues and territory was yet to be politically internalised. The dispute was over transit fee which led to SPLA occupying Panthau and a complete shutdown of oil production. In *Abyei, the CPA and the war in Sudan's New South*, Douglas H. Johnson stated that

> "The Comprehensive Peace Agreement succeeded in resolving Sudan's oldest political question regarding the future of South Sudan, but its most obvious failure was the resumption of war inside Sudan's New South along its border with South Sudan before the latter's formal independence in July 2011. By focusing on resolving the southern problem only, the international mediators failed to recognise the common political, economic, and cultural issues of marginalisation that linked large parts of the border region to the wider war. Conflict in Abyei preceded the outbreak of the Second Civil War in 1983, but the Abyei Protocol was largely an afterthought that inadequately addressed the main issues confronting the peoples of the area. The CPA as a whole failed to include robust monitoring instruments to enforce compliance, enabling Khartoum to refuse to accept any restriction to the Abyei conflict on anything but its own terms." [28]

The Abyei issue was shackled by multiple political encumbrances. It was mishandled by SPLM'S negotiating delegation,

---

28   Abyei, the CPA and the war in Sudan's new South

allowing NCP to carve it out from Southern Sudan political agenda in Machakos, in addition to mediator misappropriation by dealing with it as a separate item from Southern Sudan's political issues. But nothing was more scathing to Abyei's political fate than the anti-Ngok preposterous campaign championed by Malwal Madut and his political mentees. Bona Malwal has achieved his perennial pursuit, undermining of the Abyei political question during the incumbency of his bosom friend, President Salva Kiir Mayardit.

As a leading figure in the Southern Front, Bona's role was central in the midwifery of the Convention's agendas scheduled prior to the Round Table Conference (RTC). Southern Front held a Convention in Malakal in 1964. In that Convention SF decided the following:

> *Type of policy it should present for the future of South Sudan...and it was decided that the Southern Front should call for the right of South Sudan to self-determination. It was also decided that the political and geographical borders of South Sudan over which the South would exercise self-determination should be the borders of the three provinces of South Sudan with the North as those borders stood when Sudan became independent on January 1956. This border definition was an important part of the debate at the Malakal convention. This was so particularly because the Abboud military regime had altered some of the provincial borders between the South and the North, after the discovery of minerals in parts of South Sudan. By defining the borders, the Southern*

JOK ALOR BULABEK

*Front limited the debate over border demarcation and
at the same time denied the North claiming parts of
the South, such as Kafia Kenji, which were part of the
South before independence. It was easy for Col. Garang
and those who negotiated the CPA on behalf of South
Sudan at Naivasha, Kenya, in 2005, to simply observe
the borders between the South and the North as they
stood on 1 January 1956.[29]*

Looking at the above quote from Bona Malwal's recent book,
Abyei of the Ngok Dinka: not yet South Sudan you would understand
that Southern Front was a mere elite-led political group whose
prime aim was power sharing and did not want to comply with the
central government's policies. Limiting the definition of Southern
Sudan border to that of 1 January 1956 which elided Abyei Area
was a political myopia. Southern Front was much concerned with
what would be accepted by the north, not a fact-based historic
demand. For Bona Malwal Madut, the hunt was big as he politically managed to prey -upon the issue of Abyei.

In the same ill-written book, Bona says;

*"After the March 1965 conference, even though it was
inclusive, political enlightenment and awareness became
more prominent in South Sudan. The people of Abyei,
for example, could see that it was time to rise up and be*

---

29   Bona 2017, *Abyei of the Ngok Dinka not yet South Sudan*,
pp145-146

60

politically active. It might have been possible to incorporate
the problem of the Ngok Dinka of Abyei into the political
cause of South Sudan, considering that the South Sudan
political movement was contemplating separation, but
`real politik` was the name of the game." [30]

The statement above is a soft confession and clear evidence that Abyei's matter could have been incorporated into the structure of Southern Sudan political demands, but for some reasons best known to the conventioneers, it was de-prioritised exactly as he put it—*real politics was the name of the game.* This political misrepresentation and misdefintion of the region of Southern Sudan in SF's Convention constituted an historical document on which North–South Sudan's borders were determined. It was indeed a setback to have it as one of the references revisited during the negotiation in Machakos, Kenya in 2002. However, it's an open secret in Ngok's political circles, that Bona Malwal Madut was abstrusely behind the wheel, particularly during Machakos. And many insinuate that nomination of Salva Kiir Mayardit for leading that particular team was no accident.

After the conflict over Panthau and SPLA withdrawal from it in 2012, international community and regional bodies, particularly Ethiopia, exerted much effort to bring the two countries on board for the implementation of the outstanding issues in an amicable manner. As a result, cooperatives Agreement was signed including the management of the oil industry. But nothing relating to Abyei was discussed in that Ethiopian mediated talks.

---

30   Ibid

However, and on a separate initiative *AUHIP presented in September 2012 a proposal to the two parties outlining a mechanism for resolving Abyei's final status. This proposal was subsequently accepted by the AUPSC in October 24 as representing a fair, equitable and workable solution to the dispute.*[31] The AUPSC requested the governments of Sudan and South Sudan to negotiate over a six-week period a final status agreement on Abyei. AUPSC later endorsed the proposal as 'final and binding'. Under pressure from the international community over the lack of implementation of a number of Sudan-South Sudan agreements and the little progress on Abyei, presidents Omar al Bashir and Salva Kiir met in Addis Ababa, Ethiopia on January 2013, achieving no practical outcome.

The two heads of state agreed to reconvene to discuss Abyei's final status only if joint executive administration, legislative council, and police force were established as required by the June Temporary Agreement. The impact of tying further discussion on Abyei's final status to the establishment of these three bodies—a process that will likely be highly politicised and easy to delay—remains to be seen. The AUHIP proposal required that a referendum be held in Abyei in October 2013 to determine whether the area will become part of Sudan or South Sudan.

Despite the fact that AUPSC endorsed the AUHIP's proposal of the 21 September 2012, Sudan's Government rebuffed it intransigently on condition that provisions of June Agreement must be implemented first. Khartoum's retrograde and desultory stand stalemated the progress on Abyei. In the meantime, Bona Malwal

---

31   The Enough Project 17 January 2013, Resolving the Crisis of Abyei

Madut put it precisely to President Kiir that Abyei should not be allowed to imperil the relations between Khartoum and Juba. Adopting Bona's political stand as strategy for dealing with Abyei turned President Kiir and Ngok politicians (Kiir's Messengers) inconsistent with the promises they made.

In his letter on 9 October 2013 to the AU Commission Chairperson, President Kiir confessed that he had tried a number of times to engage his counterpart, President Bashir of Sudan with the view of agreeing to peacefully settle the Abyei's final status, but all in vain. Therefore, Kiir requested from African Union Commission to;

- Include the issue of the Abyei Area Referendum and endorsement of the AUHIP September 21st, 2012, proposal in the agenda of the upcoming AU summit of October 11th, 2013 as an urgent matter;

- That the AUPSC in an extraordinary summit, finally endorse the AUHIP proposal of September 21st, 2012;

- That without any unnecessary delay, and as provided in the AUHIP proposal, the AU Commission forms the Abyei Area Referendum Commission by appointing its chairperson

- And ask both South Sudan and Sudan to send names of their nominees in order for the Commission to commence registration of voters and conduct the Abyei Area Referendum on time in October, 2013;

- And urge the Government of Sudan to unconditionally withdraw from Kec/Diffra, to allow UNISFA full security control over the Abyei Area.

With this move, President Salva Kiir was considered to have officially surrendered the issue of Abyei to African Union and international community, then took a "laissez-faire" stand! Of course, that was in compliance with Bona Malwal Madut's esoteric project which he succeeded in convincing President Kiir to adopt as South Sudan's policy on Abyei. However, the situation in Abyei was devastating, no clear political vision of what would be next after Khartoum and Juba reached a deadlock and postponement of Abyei referendum became clearly ineluctable.

CHAPTER 7

ABYEI COMMUNITY'S REFERENDUM
(OCTOBER 2013)

A mid that dilemma and heightened political climate in Abyei, a handful of civil activists came up extemporaneously with the daring initiative to support their community which was extremely immersed in a wretched state of hopelessness. This group embarked on discussions during leisure time in Agok market and formed an informal assembly, they were thirteen in number. Members of this unique group had remarkable characteristics and extraordinary mavenry. Most of them were senior employees of the operating international organisations in the area, lawyers and senior civil servants. This group was the bud of what had subsequently been labelled as Abyei Area's Community Referendum Committee, but their move was initially an initiative for support of Abyei referendum. To have an in-depth reflection on the then compelling circumstances, I interviewed one of G13's members as quoted below;

> *For several months between April and August 2013, a group of concerned young men in Abyei spent countless hours airing their disappointments regarding the nonmoving waters of the planned October 2013 Abyei referendum. Several questions were being raised in regard to lack of movement in Juba regarding the referendum which made them wary and they decided to take things into their own hands. In July 2013, a group of young men decided to hold planning meetings. The meetings were held near Agok airstrip with two main objectives.*[32]

1. What could they do to advance the cause of the referendum?
2. What are the challenges facing the referendum? (internationally, regionally, nationally and on the ground in Abyei).

With those questions, the group of thirteen young men and women came together and strategised and came up with an action plan to address the challenges facing Abyei. After a series of deliberations, the group determined to approach the challenges through consolidating the internal front and reignite the Community's enthusiasm towards a common cause.

In order to propel the objectives forward, six steps were proposed:

---

32   Bol Biong Bol, *Challenges from within*, January 18, 2024, Entebbe

1. The first step was coordinate with Abyei civil society under the chairmanship of Dr. Rau Manyiel, to quell any possible conflict around roles and responsibilities and keep the unity of the Ngok intake.
2. The second was to raise funds for the planned a activities and marches.
3. Third was to convince the media houses locally and internationally to air the content of the marches and demonstrations globally.
4. Fourth was to write our demands to the UN security council and the African Union through UNISFA and the media.
5. Fifth was to wake up our politicians in Juba to hold press conferences in relations to the people's demands.
6. Six, to a community-organised referendum in Abyei whether supported or not.

All the six objectives were achieved, and in coordination with the CSO we united our mission to stage the demonstrations which were attended by more than 20,000 people as reported by UNISFA and the media houses.

The community's demands were communicated to the international community right from ground zero in Abyei, the politicians held press conferences, people were transported from across South Sudan to Abyei, the community referendum was completed successfully despite threats from the Misseriya to attack. However, it is worth mentioning that several challenges were observed which are highlighted below. However, despite the unwavering determination of our people amid monumental external obstacles, the internal challenges within our own ranks played a paramount role in our quest for success.

I bore witness to the frustration of our people, often directed towards Juba and, more specifically, Abyei elites. This sentiment was not to be dismissed lightly; it arose from legitimate concerns that demanded immediate collective attention. One prominent issue contributing to internal strife was the profound detachment between the elites and the masses, exemplified by the stark contrast between Abyei elites in Juba heights and the masses in the slums of Abyei. This disconnect stemmed from feeble relationship, fueled by a lack of interest or concern in involving the ground-level population in decision-making processes at the centre. For example, several committees were formed, plans were drawn, all ostensibly in the name of the people on the ground, yet without meaningful investment in the committees or consultations. This gave rise to mistrust and a lack of confidence, perpetuating the illusion that only Juba elites held the reins of Abyei destiny.

This stark mistrust was manifested in the absence of coordination and the inconsiderate decisions made by the elites to the extent that the majority of all the referendum and the return committees were ninety-nine percent from Juba. Not only that, but the committee members who mobilised the people for the referendum were brought from Juba, disregarding the role played by the initiators to mobilise more than 20,000 to march despite the terrible seasonal conditions and the distance people walked for their cause. Dismissively, the elites' mobilisation committee from Juba, came on the ground less than a month before the referendum to assemble the public who were already activated without involving the common people's committee (Michar Ageer). This move demonstrated a lack of consideration for the work already done on the ground and highlighted the disregard for the contributions of the common man (Michar Ageer) in Abyei.

To further argue, the process of return amplified these concerns. Committees in Juba, including the Abyei task force and Abyei high-level referendum committee, failed to communicate with the people on the ground or share their objectives. Oversight and supervision mechanisms were notably absent, resulting in a lack of coordination and communication. This neglect damaged the relationship between Juba and Abyei, hindering progress rather than fostering collaboration. Nonetheless, building a robust, sound, and united front for the greater good required strategic planning, coordination of efforts and consolidation of resources. But ignoring the contributions of the people on the ground only deepened existing wounds. It is best to discard the illusion that makes those working in Juba superior to those residing in the slums of Abyei. The mixed feelings our people harboured towards our elites, who often seemed distant and indifferent, created a bitter-sweet dynamic that needed urgent resolution. In delivering this message, my intention was not to fall on deaf ears or be taken personally. It was a reflection of the sentiments, observations, and experiences on the ground. Acknowledging that the term "elites" might be unjust and "Juba" too general, the central message remained clear—the inclusivity in all our endeavors, guided by the principle of *by the people and for the people.* The past presented an opportune moment for us to bridge the gaps, heal the wounds, and unite for a brighter future.

CHAPTER 8

REACTIONS ON ABYEI COMMUNITY'S REFERENDUM

"The Government of South Sudan is not a part of the activities ongoing in Abyei. What is happening is the work of a pressure group."

- Michael Makuei Lueth

When youth elites and some elements from Abyei's Civil Society in Juba observed that their counterparts on the ground (Abyei's Youth Union and Civil Society Organisations) were consistently and persistently moving on with mobilisation of the masses for the referendum, they decided to get on the stage in the eleventh hour. Most of those youth were former African National Front's (ANF) activists in the Sudanese Universities. With their political and organisational consciousness, they decided to call in some of their former ANF's comrades from other regions of South Sudan in order to add to the process some nationalistic flavour. Hence, the chair of National Youth's Committee for the Referendum of Abyei was given to late Victor Thomas who hails from Bari ethnicity of Jebel Lado of Central Equatoria.

Deciphering the errant nature of Abyei referendum's process requires a thorough probe. Unfortunately, key players who were in charge are not ready to help in unveiling the nitty-gritty of what had exactly transpired. One of the eeriest sides of Abyei referendum was how it possibly turned into a government agent-controlled initiative, while it was primarily a byproduct of ordinary people's determination. Heavyweight political elements from Abyei got their way to it, names such as Deng Alor Kuol, Chol Deng Alak, and others had in one way or another become active planners of the process!

As mentioned in Bol B. Bol's statement, key positions and structural functions were notably dominated by Juba-based cabals and monotonous names such as Romano Kuot had his mighty hands on the secretariat. Despite the fact that this work was primarily initiated by conscience-driven grassroot campaigners, the G13, none of them was seen to have been assigned in any of the key positions in Abyei referendum structures. Lucrative committees such as that of mobilisation and transportation were dominantly occupied by Ngok's Juba-based political camarillas and economic parasitic cartels.

The other most shady aspects of the referendum were its sources of finance and the controversial malpractices rumoured around it.

Referendum assets were said to have been divided right away and some were still driving those prestigious vehicles until recent times. Due to the equivocal nature of this project, tracing its transactions became difficult, particularly the financial ones. It was not clear whether it was funded by the Ministry of Finance, Presidency or through Ngok's related networks of cartels!

However, South Sudan's Minister of Information, Michael Makuei Lueth has disclosed recently in the 7th Governor's Conference, during his inimical exchange with Abyei's Chief Administrator, Chol Deng Alak, that Abyei referendum was solely financed by the Government of South Sudan. Nevertheless, it remains bogglesome why the Government of South Sudan injected huge resources into a referendum it would not recognize.

Conversely, Khartoum continued its arm-twisting policy by threatening the Government of South Sudan not to involve in a unilateral referendum in the contested region of Abyei. Sudan's Foreign Ministry spokesperson, Abu Bakr al Sideeg described holding a unilateral referendum as *Warbling away from the flock and a breach of the cooperation agreements.*[33] Moreover, Sudan's head of the Sub-committee on Legislation and Justice, Al Fadil Haj Suleiman, announced Sudan's absolute rejection for holding Abyei Referendum in October and warned of doing so without involving the Arab Misseriya tribesmen, stating that it would be an invalid move. Despite the unwavering stand of the African Union

---

33   Sudan's Foreign Ministry Spokesperson, Abu Bakr Sideeg. https// sudaneseonline.com/cgi_bin//esdb/2bb/cgi https://www.eyeradio.org/sudan_ declare_position_abyei_referendum/?amp

High Implementation Panel (AUHIP) that permanent settlers of the Abyei region, the Ngok Dinka are the only eligible voters, Khartoum intransigently insisted that Misseriya must be involved in the process. From the abovementioned statement, it's apparent that Khartoum was strategic in the issue of Abyei and why sovereign institutions such as National parliament and Ministry of Foreign Affairs got involved directly.[34]

Shortly before the slated month for Abyei referendum, South Sudan's president Salva Kiir Mayardit wrote to the African Union Commission (AUC) saying he saw no possibility of reaching an understanding with Khartoum over the disputed region anytime soon, even if discussions continued for 100 years. In the letter, Kiir urged the continental body to take complete responsibility for the impasse between the two countries. To rescue the situation and save Kiir's face after his despondent statement, James Wani Igga announced on the state-owned Television (SSTV) that South Sudan would stand with the people of Abyei: *We will not give up, we will never surrender and we want to assure you that we will not let Abyei down. Never, ever will the government and the people of South Sudan turn their backs.*[35]

Surprisingly, South Sudan said that it is not supporting the conduct of a unilateral referendum. Michael Makuei Lueth, South Sudan's Minister of Information said;

---

34   Sudan's head of the sub-committee on Legislation and Justice, Al Fadil Haj Suleiman. https//sudaneseonline.com/cgi_bin/esdb/2bb_cgi

35   Vice President, James Wani Igga statement on SSTV. https://reliefweb.int/report/south_sudan_republic

"The government of South Sudan is not a part of the activities ongoing in Abyei. What is happening there is the work of the pressure group. It is the work of the Civil Society from Abyei. It is the people of Abyei who are doing that, not the government of South Sudan. Speaking in a press conference, Makuei questioned how a unilateral vote could help break the deadlock over the future of Abyei if the result was not formally recognised by either Sudan or South Sudan. Michael Makuei Lueth continued by saying Can they [the people of Abyei] do that without Sudan and South Sudan? Even if it has to be an independent State, it needs to be recognised." [36]

Looking at how contradictory the South Sudanese leaders' statements were, compared to those of their counterparts, the Sudanese, you would understand that South Sudan has no national agreed-upon policy on Abyei. There was an apparent lack of coherence, top senior officials of the land, the President, Vice President and Spokesperson of the Central Government shouldn't be incoherent as such. All their stated stands above prove beyond doubt that South Sudan had never had a strategic, resolute position on the issue of Abyei.

The only genuine reaction was of late hero, Edward Lino Abyei who said;

---

36   Information Minister, Michael Makuei Lueth. https://relief-web.int/report/south_sudan_sudan_republic/south_sudan_rejects_unilateral_referendum_vote_abyei

"The only way to resolve this conflict is through referendum. The international community should now stand with the people of Abyei who for decades have been subjected to suffering and killing, but did not give up because they were hoping that the world would one day stand with them. This patience is no longer holding simply because the more people wait, the more their condition gets worsened on the watch of the international community."[37]

Edward Lino's political reading was so accurate, I wished he could have made it up to the year 2022, to see how his people were preyed upon by their own kinfolk! He was literally right, the more people wait, the more their conditions get ravaged.

The result of Abyei people's referendum was not a surprise when 99.98% voted in favour of joining South Sudan. It had been Ngok's chief dream to rejoin their kinfolk in the South. However, ordinary people were shocked seeing a government of the country which they sacrificed a great deal to exist, denying them in that opprobrious manner. Despite the severity of that disappointment which surely disheartened Ngok community, they still believe it was the right decision and if given another chance to vote, they shall unfailingly choose to join South Sudan, because this is where they originally belong.

---

37   Edward Lino statement on the Abyei referendum. https://reliefweb.int/report/south_sudan_republic/south_sudan_rejects_unilateral_referendum_vote_abyei

PART 4

POST-BELLUM SOUTH SUDAN

"Government is only an executive control, a centralised authority for the purpose of expressing the will of the people. Before you have a government, you must have the people. Without the people there can be no government, the government must be, therefore an expression of the will of the people."

- Marcus Garvey

CHAPTER 9

THE EPHEMERAL JOY

I was in Juba in that historic moment, 9 July 2011, when South Sudan's flag swayed gently for the first time at Dr. John Garang Mausoleum. It was ineffable, people were incredibly elated. Some were crying, others cheerfully dancing. People flocked from everywhere at every street marching towards the venue, that sense of togetherness and homogeneity is very hard to be restored. On that great day, the irresistible voice of the young talented artist, Kang J J was joyfully dominating.

"We are free at last!"

This day shall indelibly remain in South Sudan people's collective memory. It is momentously called in Konyo-konyo simple Arabic (Yom Ar`fau A'lam), which can loosely be translated as Independence Day.

The infrastructural capacities of the new capital (Juba) were far behind the event, there were no roads or suitable enough hotels in Juba to accommodate the guests from worldwide. Members of the international community representing their states and global organisations were present and very active in the scene. United Nations, United States of America, African Union, IGAD, Norway, Kenya, Uganda and all state and non-state friends to the people of Southern Sudan who directly or sympathetically supported the Liberation were happy because their efforts yielded fruits at last. July 9, 2011 saw a newly autonomous South Sudan proclaim her republican status after seceding from Sudan at the peak of a long and tortuous emancipation process facilitated by international organisations and conscientious foreign governments. South Sudan was first of all admitted to the UN General Assembly on recommendation of the Security Council, then to African Union membership later that month. [38]

People were all hope and had numerous dreams. Leadership of Post-independence South Sudan disappointed the hoi polloi, hence, all their deserved aspirations for peace, stability and development despairingly poured into the ocean of unknown. South Sudanese seceded, but their collective memory was still obsessed with State's political maltreatment and exploitation which they

---

38   *Building Peace in Africa: reviewing the international framework to resolve Abyei final status between Sudan and South Sudan*, Onyekochi Obi-Okoye. US, Italy, Norway and UK recommended South Sudan be granted membership in the United Nations, UN Security Council Res.1990/2011

experienced for decades before and after the independence of Sudan. For people of South Sudan the dream was big, they for the first time felt first class citizens in a country of their own and thought no one shall be again discriminated against, based on regional, ethnic or political affiliation. Moreover, issues of uneven development, social injustice and inequitable distribution of opportunities were part of tribulations and political grudges that caused Southerners to revolt against the central Governments, therefore, people were hugely expecting change be exigently brought about.

According to Garvey's definition, government's purpose is to express the people's will and that people should be put superior to Governments. Establishing cohesive communities with common ideals should have been made a priority in order to found a country that could become sustainable. Since time immemorial, peoples of Southern Sudan had never been under a direct centralised authority, they were separate entities governed by native administrations and Sultanates. No structural linkages between them, neighbouring communities were mostly bound by conflicts over grazing zones, water sources or any other means of livelihood.

It is an indisputable fact, South Sudanese had never been one people, whether before or after 1972's regional government. Government's essence was only sensed by elites and town's residents such as Juba, Wau and Malakal, but ordinary people remained disengaged and knew little about each other's cultures. Generally, Southern Sudan became a quasi-political society starting from the Liberation periods, in limited scale during Anya-Nya One from 1960s to 1972. However, largish politicisation was achieved by Sudan People's Liberation Movement which made an extensive revolutionary call and was acutely responded to from all over the region of Southern Sudan and beyond, particularly by students, government officials and labourers of marginal works (Jungo).

From SPLA's literature, ethnic consciousness is strongly notice-able and that was due to its establishment's factors. Recruits were not enlisted the way it is often done by official armies. It was an optional response, therefore, orientational degree varied from one group to another. Armed groups that existed before the movement (SPLM/A) were of pure tribal and regional nature, and from them, SPLA rudimentary units were formed. This passive ethnic aware-ness was used opportunistically for factional mobilisation during SPLA internal feuds and had resulted in devastating inveterate experiences that are hard to politically internalise. Thousands of Southern Sudanese civil populace flocked together and joined the revolution from different corners motivated by various grievances which were seemingly different from one region to another. For instance, areas along the north-south border such as Awiel, Abyei, Wau and Warrap, apart from SAF brutality, were facing Maraheel force which was mainly formed out of Misseriya and Reziegat. These nomadic tribes were instrumentalised by Sudan central governments and used as suppressive forces against Southern Sudanese civil populations at South-North borders.

The primary intent of many youth from those areas was to get arms to defend their own villages. Moreover, residents of towns such as Juba, Wau and Malakal were subjected to gross human rights violations by SAF and mujahedeen. Those religion-oriented fighters used force unscrupulously against innocent civilians and that pushed many to join the SPLA despite the risk it involved.

So immediate motives that forced people to join the SPLA may look slightly different from one place to another, but there was something in common, the offender. Southern Sudanese of different categories shared repugnance towards northern Sudan due to exploitation and political marginalisation practised by its elites. This was how the spirit of togetherness came about and served as the foundation for South Sudan Nationalism. *The idea of South Sudan as a nation and the struggle to achieve its independence were defined from a negative point: the South's antagonism towards North Sudan as an enemy. The enemy became the common denominator of the sense of nation shared by all of its 64 ethnicities.*[39]

As described in the beginning of this chapter, people were blissful for the independence, because they did sacrifice dearly by offering food and their dear sons and daughters. Dr. Garang hired no mercenaries from foreign countries, but children of all Southern Sudan's tribes were instrumentalised for the Liberation. I really feel sorry when seeing ordinary people being derided as if they were not participants in the Liberation of this country. Yes, wars were fought, but the final status was realised after people practised their civic rights and overwhelmingly voted for secession.

Because they believed it was a product of their armed and civil struggles, South Sudanese irrespective of their regions, ethnicities and sections, had proudly owned the achievement of the country. This could have been judiciously used as a concrete foundation for state and nation building. Unfortunately, Kiir and his peers epitomized the Arabic adage which says; *a container smells as exactly as*

---

39   Peter Adwok, *South Sudan endless war,* p9

what it contains. SPLM leaders had deep-seated acrimony towards each other which resulted in unnecessary, destructive infighting.

On that evening 15 December 2013, I was at Paradise Hotel in Yirol sitting in front of my room browsing on Facebook. Then I observed that people were frightened, so I decided to call a friend of mine who was a member of SPLM's National Liberation Council (NLC) to enquire about the situation in Juba. He confirmed it to me in Dinka language: *Baai a ce paath*, meaning the situation is not fine. Rumours were controversially circulated about who did what that led to cracking of the first bullet. However, such happenstances could not develop into a pervasive war unless there were clandestine saboteurs who promoted it to achieve their goals. The most devastating form of conflict is the political one among various leaders fighting for power, whether at the national or state level. Unfortunately, sometimes politicians play the ethnic card, drawing their tribes into conflict against the other. In this sense, the last two trends, the ethnic composition of the country and the political rivalries, are interlinked, and they are at the root of what has been happening in Juba and South Sudan since December 15, 2013.[40]

The war which was perpetually fought in South Sudan after the independence has nothing to do with ordinary citizens and unarmed political forces, it was exclusively SPLM's. Instead of founding the country on justice, equality, freedom and democratic ideals, SPLM's leaders unethically embarked on an internal power struggle using ethnicity as a tool. Reverting the people of South

40   *The South Sudan: A political rivalry that turned ethnic*, Ciprian Sandu 7, April 2014

Sudan to war again in less than three years proved that SPLM's misleaders were just after power. Reputedly, SPLM leadership has lost legitimacy, because it was entirely centered around Liberation's objectives which they have been subverting. *Since the outbreak of war in December 2013, up to two million people have left South Sudan, abandoning their homes and crossing the nearest border to safety. More than 200,000 people now live in the UN-protected camps inside South Sudan. Millions more are internally displaced.*[41]

By plunging the people of South Sudan again into war dehumanising conditions which they had been exposed to for decades under Riverine Elite's Neo-colonialism, many envisaged SPLM's government as a flipside of Sudan's previous administrations.

> *Our people were naively misled to turn against objectivity. How could a movement like the SPLM/SPLA, which led the people for twenty-two years, turn against the people whom it liberated in such an inhumane way, in a matter of three years? How can a movement, which confronted tribalism for more than twenty years begin to preach and kill people based on tribalism and other sorts of negativisms, planned by "aliens " for reasons unknown to the SPLM/SPLA?*[42]

---

41   *Ethnocide as a tool of State-building: South Sudan and the never-ending war*, Dr. Carol Berger

42   Edward Lino Abyei, *Dr. John Garang de Mabior A man to know* page 31

CHAPTER 10

SPLM'S INFIGHTING
IMPACT ON ABYEI

As mentioned earlier, the independence of South Sudan was achieved through a multifaceted deal which seriously devastated the Abyei political cause. This deal on Abyei was unfortunately done behind the people, between SPLM leadership and the Government of Sudan. The political gain in the deal (Postponement of Abyei referendum), as propagated was to allow the ultimate goal, the independence of Southern Sudan be achieved and that had repeatedly been messaged to the populace in Abyei. After the independence, instead of pursuing the liberation unfinished agendas, namely Abyei, borders, oil and distribution of assets, SPLM leadership shortsightedly fueled an unnecessary power feud which brought about total destruction and uncalled-for humanitarian disasters. Hence, all outstanding issues which should have been championed by post-indepen-dence's government were badly disregarded. Deng Alor Kuol, a quondam Minister of South Sudan Foreign Affairs and a veteran politician from Abyei whose name for decades has been used almost interchangeably with the Abyei political cause, was among the defected groups—the Former Detainees (FDs) or (G10)—as subsequently labelled. Alor's defection was met with heteroge-neous reactions within and outside Abyei community. That of course has nothing to do with him as a person, but Abyei political status and its implications.

It is widely believed that resolution of the Abyei question had never been a priority for the Government of South Sudan, there-upon, people of Abyei could have possibly become beneficiaries of that change. Alor's move was met with mixed reactions, not because of opposing Kiir, but due to imprecision of his defection's agenda. Ngok envisaged him as he who was barking up the wrong tree. On the flipside, critics of Ngok's political leadership viewed him (Deng Alor) as an outlandish participant in the power struggle of a country that does not fully recognise him as a citizen. As for the people of Abyei, many wanted not only Deng Alor, but most of Ngok veterans to have joined the opposition and declare the dereliction of Abyei issue as a grievance.

Despite the fact that Abyei leaders, except Deng Alor and Edward Lino, whether in political or militaristic institutions, were in Kiir's camp or muted, Bona Malwal Madut insisted on pursuing his unslakable depravity, by infusing the president's mind with malicious advice to harass Ngok's leaders and undermine the political cause of Abyei Area.

Bona's animus against the people of Abyei is one-of-a-kind, he mastered it successfully as demonstrated in his statement below.

When an individual feels he has all the power in his hands, there is nothing that he feels he cannot do. So it was with Deng Alor Kuol and the gang of his cousins and friends from Abyei. No constraints and the feeling of being ever-powerful had led to the leaders of Abyei within the SPLM machine in South Sudan feeling that every power was theirs) .(In the last reshuffle of the military and political leadership of the SPLA, General Pieng Deng Kuol became chief of the national police of South Sudan. It is never stated in the South Sudanese system of government why changes like this are made. But if the idea was to move him away from the army, to ease the confrontation with Khartoum over Abyei, because he was always visiting Abyei with a mighty force, then nothing has changed. In the SPLM system, the military and the police force are equally potent forces. However, at the time of writing, Lieutenant General Pieng Deng Kuol had been removed from his new post. It would appear that some political upheaval has afflicted the Deng Majok Kuol Arop family within the SPLM political establishment as a result of their dubious role in the attempted coup in Juba on 15 December 2015, which attempted to overthrow the elected government.[43]

Bona's unstanchable turpitude and his insatiable impunity towards Abyei and its people, requires no savoir-faire to conclude that he was the schemer of most of the political woes inflicted on the people of Abyei in South Sudan. As result of his influence,

---

43   Bona 2017

Abyei leaders were elbowed out of South Sudan's National Governments. This is what he said again:

> *"The third and the last of Deng Majok Kuol Arop's children I mentioned in the earlier part of this chapter, and who also plays a role in the misuse of the power of South Sudan in the name of the people of Abyei, is Luka Biong Deng Majok Kuol Arop. As part of the powerful gang from Abyei, he was a powerful player in the name of South Sudan in the relationship between Khartoum and Juba, a relationship that has now come to serious loggerheads."* [44]

Bona Malwal Madut's objective was indubitably mischievous, his pertinacious political stand against Ngok people of Abyei is tantamount to discrimination on sectional basis. Bona tried his best to antagonise not only governments of Warrap and Juba, but South Sudan as a whole against the people of Abyei by mirroring their political cause as a problem. Following Deng Alor's defection, anti-Ngok saboteurs were blabbering to their demigods at (J1) that Abyei matter should not be pursued while Deng Alor did mutiny against the Government! In the Sudanese culture, this sort of uncouth justification is called *an excuse which is uglier than the guilt.*

It was a very lame justification and a direct connivance, because Abyei is an impersonal question, no matter how much that person

---

44   Ibid

was attached to it. However, Abyei file was assigned to Justice Deng Biong Mijak, but no apparent political development was observed. Of course, it was not about who was able to achieve what; rather, the way J1's leadership wanted the issue of Abyei to be dealt with. To make sure it was brought under control for the mutual interest of Sudan and South Sudan, Abyei file was assigned to one of Omar Al-Bashir's former Jack of all trades, Tut Gatluak Manime who doubled as Kiir's adviser on National Security Affairs. The committee was established when operationalisation of R-ARCISS kicked off in May 2021. The cited terms of reference for the committee were to;

- *Pursue the final status of the Abyei Area through engagement with the Government of the Republic of the Sudan;*
- *Present the position of the Government of the Republic of South Sudan to the Government of Republic of the Sudan, the United Nations, the African Union including other multilateral partners, by reflecting the spirit of the Comprehensive Peace Agreement (CPA) 2005 and other relevant resolutions or documentations on the final status of Abye;*
- *Advise the Government of the Republic of South Sudan on necessary steps towards realisation of the final status of Abyei Area.*[45]

45   Republican order No.22/2022/ reconstitution of Abyei file's Committee

This committee was reconstituted by creating a sub-committee on Development of Natural Resources which, according to its terms of reference, was authorised to pursue the following;

- *To create a cooperation framework for the development of oil and other natural resources in the Abyei Area pursuant to the joint presidential Communique of 18th March 2022, with respect to cooperation along the borders of the two independent countries through the development of untapped resources such as oilfields and agricultural land;*
- *To engage with the communities to ensure their participation and outreach to international partners in development of oil and other natural resources in the Abyei Area;*
- *And to liaise and work closely with the Ministry of Petroleum and any other relevant Government institution, which shall provide the Sub-Committee with all necessary guidance in any petroleum or agricultural sector engagement.*

However, insiders depicted that move as a political tactic to bamboozle the public and drive their attention away from self-rule proposal which heated the political atmosphere following its adoption in September 2022 by a majority of Abyei's people and remains the popular political demand up to this time of writing. The reconstitution of Abyei file's committee was met *with arriére-pensée* due to time irrelevancy and the way Abyei's oil had been managed before and after the independence of South Sudan. The Agreement on the Resolution of Abyei Conflict (Abyei Protocol) which was signed in Naivasha, Kenya May 26th, 2004 article (3) states the following;

> *3.1 Without prejudice to the provisions of the Wealth Sharing Agreement, the net-oil revenue from the oil produced in Abyei Area shall be shared during the interim period as follows:*
> *3.1.1 Fifty Percent (50%) to the National Government;*
> *3.1.2 Forty Two Percent (42%) to the Government of Southern Sudan;*
> *3.1.3 Two Percent (2%) to Bahar el Ghazal Region;*
> *3.1.4 Two Percent (2%) to Western Kordofan;*
> *3.1.5 Two Percent (2%) locally with the Ngok Dinka;*
> *3.1.6 Two Percent (2%) locally with the Misseriya People.*[46]

It is worth mentioning that Ngok people of Abyei had never participated in the management of the oil produced in their region, and the whereabout of their percentage (2%) was completely veiled. However, article (3.1) clearly indicates that the oil produced in Abyei shall be shared during the interim period, so new arrangements were required after the independence of Southern Sudan. It is therefore bogglesome why South Sudan established such an advance technical committee at national level

---

46   Abyei Protocol

for Abyei oil's management without proper consideration to the final political status of the area! Neither the political section of the committee which is now three years old, nor its recently established sub-committee for resources development did achieve any tangible advancement.

In a lengthy interview with Wuor Mijak, a political analyst and Abyei SPLM's long-served Secretary for Information, Mijak admitted that the SPLM internal rift had seriously affected the political status of Abyei Area.

Many people from Abyei have despondently concluded that the final resolution of their political question won't be achieved during Kiir's incumbency. However, Ngok's political elites should consider how to advocate for, and make the people of South Sudan better understand the issue of Abyei. When I shortly made it to the Revitalized Transitional National Legislative Assembly (R-TNLA), I realised that a range of South Sudanese politicians were misinformed. It is, therefore, significant to instill Abyei in people's hearts and make them conscious of the territorial dispute over it with Sudan. I believe in our generation's ability, despite the damages inflicted on them by this draconian system which used economic deprivation as a political tool, things wont be the same if they takeover.

Those who studied in the Sudanese universities from the early nineties up to the independence of Southern Sudan were without doubt revolutionised and wholeheartedly supported the struggle from within. Youths were ardently engaged in many student political organisations such as ANF, UDSF, UDF etc, while others scattered in some northern political forums such as

Sudanese Communist Party (SCP). Such generations with unparalleled political consciousness and know-how could have been used for development. Deplorably, Kiir's opprobrious government perceived them as potential threats, not value added. However, and in spite of all the uncountable political obstructions, I am optimistic, and my only advice to South Sudanese young people generally and Abyei's in particular is to never say die, the unfeigned liberty which we all aspired for will inevitably come.

PART 5

LEFT IN THE LURCH

"To me the thing that is worse than death is betrayal."

- Malcolm X

CHAPTER 11

SOLD OUT
IN THE ELEVENTH HOUR!

The chief architect of the scheme vowed not to hose down before he achieved his stanchless desire. He was quoted instigating the youth of his section saying; *You should claim your land while I am still alive, because if I die, you won't be able to realise it.*[47] Bona Malwal tried hard to put to use his political influence on South Sudan's President to realise his ill-dream which he devoted much of his adulthood's energy to achieving. South Sudan's version of NCP's like-minded politicians were conscious of SPLM current leadership's position on Abyei, hence manipulatively used that knowledge as exactly did their cohorts in the north.

Since CPA's implementation period up to the independence

---

47   Lt. Gen. Kuol Diem Kuol's report before the Council of States 2022

of Southern Sudan, SPLM leadership had been blind as a bat compromising on Abyei Protocol. This turned many people incredulous and concluded that there might have been a collusion between the interlinked systems in Sudan and South Sudan to divide Abyei. Apparently, Sudan did early embark on this strategy using Misseriya as a political shield. This scheme, as mentioned by Wour Mijak, had been backed by Sudan's security forces presence at the oilfield of Langer (Difra), and also benefited from UNISFA's misappropriation of the Quick Impact Project Funds (QIP) for Misseriya's settlement in the northern part of Abyei region.

The Agreement on the Resolution of Abyei Conflict (Abyei Protocol) signed in Naivasha, Kenya 26th, 2004 article (1.2.1) states that; *Residents of Abyei will be citizens of both Western Kordofan and Bahar el Ghazl, with representation in the legislatures of both states*. That was the political and legal status of Abyei before the independence of Southern Sudan, it was under presidency of Sudan which was comprised of President Omar al Bashir of National Congress Party and Salva Kiir Mayardit of Sudan People's Liberation Movement as First Vice President. After CPA in 2005, Abyei Area ceased to be solely considered a northern territory, but a shared area between Northern and Southern Sudan pending the final status. In May, two months before the declaration of the independence of Southern Sudan, NCP tactically invaded Abyei to impose a de facto situation.

Consequently, June Agreement was demandingly signed in Addis Ababa to facilitate the independence of Southern Sudan. The Agreement for Temporary Administrative and Security Arrangements was compliantly negotiated with intention to encounter NCP's tendency aimed at hindering the independence process. However, one provision only was implemented: the deployment of UN forces [UNISFA]_ but the rest, such as formation of executive and legislative councils and police units, were not materialised due to Ngok principled rejection to any sort of Joint administration that would again invite Misseriya into their political affairs.

Putatively, Abyei Area was de-linked from Sudan before the independence of Southern Sudan when President Omar Al-Bashir unilaterally annulled its administration following the second invasion in May 2011. In addition to that, people of Abyei, like other southerners, lost citizenship in Sudan when Sudan's parliament passed the bill for revocation of citizenship from all South Sudanese shortly before the independence. (Later Sudan's Government did wickedly exempt the people of Abyei for political purposes). Thus, Abyei Area remained for years without any constitutionally appointed administration. It was run by bureaucrats and traditional administration (Chiefs) which was the only recognised authority by UN and other international organisations.

I wonder, when seeing some politicians driven by hatred derisively labelled Abyei as Kordofan territory! Abyei is politically an area of limited statehood, it is neither Sudan nor South Sudan. Neither of the two countries has full authority to practise sovereignty over it. However, Abyei has its internationally=recognised territory defined as an area of the nine Ngok Dinka Chiefdoms whose people are entitled to vote in a referendum to determine the future of their area. But Bona Malwal Madut vowed to estrange Abyei, give it to Sudan where he was rewarded with appointment as a presidential advisor during the CPA interim period, though he was not known to be a member of Sudan's NCP ruling party!

To achieve his lifetime's mission, Bona Malwal Madut recruited from all over Twic community some stiff-necked, bigoted politicians he used as tools for the realisation of his agenda. One of the very enthusiastic protégés of Bona's policies (Bonaism) is Charles Majak Aleer, a member of South Sudan National Legislative Assembly who doubles as a member of Jieng Council of Elders (JCE).

In 2015, a strange, uncalled-for fragmentation was made on the national structure of the country, when Kiir's Administration redivided South Sudan on ethnic basis, a trickery believed to have been a brainchild of JCE. Unfortunately, Abyei was included in that cantonisation when President Salva Kiir Mayardit ordered the establishment of Abyei Special Administrative Area on 18 February 2015 (ASAA/ Order No. 3/2015). As result, Abyei was carved out from Warrap State and given its separate administrative unit. This move was hopefully welcomed by Abyei's people considering it a sort of recognition from the government of South Sudan, though it was put under the office of the president.

This deceptive contrivance was swiftly done before cantonisation to be seen as isolated from it. But after 2022 conspiratory episodes, many concluded that detaching Abyei from Warrap was just a threshold. It could have become a paradox to claim an area which was already part of their territory. Abyei Special Administrative Area's creation was a fore story of the scheme.

In *Ethnocide as a Tool of State-building: South Sudan and the Never-ending War* Dr. Carol Berger mentioned the following;

"Members of the Twic Dinka have been accused of seeking to annex some parts of the Abyei Area to the newly created Twic State. This includes Dinka Ngok land that lies South of the river Kiir. In particular, Charles Majak, the chair of the special Jieng Council committee struck to revise the states of South Sudan, has been named as responsible for the attempts, which he has denied. Bona Malual, a Twic Dinka and also a member of the Jieng Council, is said to be behind the lobbying to claim Ngok Dinka land. Further to the unresolved status of Abyei, Malwal has even published a book on the matter, Abyei of the Ngok Dinka: Not Yet South Sudan (2017). For decades he has claimed that Abyei belongs to Sudan. The effective ceding of territory in the disputed Abyei region to Sudan, northernmost Greater Bahar el Ghazl, is not unrelated to the wider campaign to depopulate non-Dinka areas and shift Dinka populations into those areas. As discussed in this paper, key individuals within the Jieng Council of Elders, and President Salva Kiir himself, have strong ties to Khartoum. Their apparent surrender of control over Abyei is consistent with the favouring of Dinka from Greater Bahar el Ghazl, particularly the Twic, who have been lobbying to take part of the Abyei territory from Abyei's historic residents, the Ngok Dinka." [48]

---

48   Dr. Carol Berger, *Ethnocide as a tool for State building*, pp14 & 41

What was mentioned in Dr. Carol's paper above has been typically taking place in Abyei Area since February 2022 up to this time of writing. The self-aggrandising Jieng Council of Elders had, through the influence of Bona Malwal Madut and his bosom friend Charles Majak Aleer, compromised Abyei in that big political mess-up. Furthermore, President Salva Kiir and his government in Juba turned a blind eye on the incursion made by Sudan into Ngok's areas and was now repeating the same with Twic's claims over Ngok lands south of the river Kiir. This was how the scornful derision of *Ngok must be driven to the river* came about. The stratagem was to yield the northern part of Abyei to Khartoum and Juba would take the southern part using an adjacent community to Ngok from the South which is Twic of Warrap State. That was the demanding circumstances which moved the young talented artist Deng Mijok Ajak Nyang. When he realised that his people were facing existential threats, he rebreathed in them the spirit of resistance to withstand that conspiracy through his wholeheartedly expressed verses; *Ngok shall never go to the sea. Ngok shall inexpugnably exist on their land, whether you like it or not, (Wic wala ce wic).*[49]

Bona Malwal Madut's conspiratorial write-ups served as theoretical sources where his epigones in Twic contrived their bogus claims over the ownership of Ngok historic lands. This ill-thought-out plan was plotted carefully when Twic got its own State which they first tried to call "Kiir State", despite the fact that there is no Kiir in Twic's territory, but "Lol River"! However, the first

---

49   Popular song of Ngok Dinka renowned artist Deng Mijok Ajak Nyang (Wic wala ce wic).

official administrative attempt ever made after South Sudan independence, was during the tenure of Twic's State Governor Kon Manyiel Kuol who directly wrote to President Kiir as precisely mentioned in the Council of States report. *The committee found out that the letter written by Hon. Kon Manyiel Kuol, the former governor of Twic State to H.E, Gen. Salva Kiir Mayardit, the President of the Republic of South Sudan, on January/30/2018, that if the Abyei box is not corrected then, it shall cause clans/communal conflict over some areas at South of River Kiir at any time. This was one of the incitements for Twic community to fight against Ngok.*[50] Same attempts were also made during the governorship of Atem Madut Yak who sent his administrators to Marol Diil of Rumamer County and Athony of Alal County with Twic State's flag.

> *"Ngok and Twic Dinka are historically very close. Friction only emerged in 2017, when the Abyei Area Administration (AAA) began a land registry in Aneet, a bustling market near Agok, in Southern Abyei. The Twic Dinka denounced the land registry, which was subsequently halted. The putative reason for this discontent was that some Twic Dinka claimed that Agok and Aneet are located within Twic County, Warrap State. The Ngok Dinka, however, consider the boundaries of Abyei to have been determined by a decision of the Permanent Court of Arbitration in The Hague in 2009, and Agok and Aneet to be part of their territory. The*

---

50   South Sudan Council of States Ad hoc Committee's Report

Twics' claim to these territories is very recent in origin and is not actually about long-standing territorial disagreement, but rather an attempt to control Aneet Market and the humanitarian hub in Agok, where many international NGOs based themselves following SAF's invasion of Abyei. The Twic saw the weakness of Ngok Dinka as an opportunity. Agok's status as a humanitarian hub and the tax base offered by Aneet have provided a source of income for the AAA. Twic County has seen almost no development." [51]

According to Dr. Joshua Craze above, real drivers of the conflict between Ngok and Twic are socio-economic. Dr. Craze's conclusion is noticeably matching with Twic authority's outlaw practices which between 2018 and 2019 imposed unlawful presence in Athony and Agok disguised as National Customs Authority. All these unseemly and irresponsible behaviors happened, though Chief Administrator of the day, Mulana Kuol Alor Kuol was so cooperative and supportive to Twic state, particularly during its establishment. Moreover, Gen. Aieu Ayeny Aleu mentioned it in his statement to Aneet Intercommunal Investigation Committee that; The taxes from Aneet Market are only benefitting Ngok Community, he stated that Twic community felt marginalised and not represented in the National Government.

Ostensibly, there were some other secondary factors which

---

51   *Attacks from both sides: Abyei existential dilemmas,* Joshua Craze July 2023

indirectly contributed to the escalation of the Ngok-Twic communal feud; amongst them the internal rifts between some Bul Nuer social sections, armed groups (SSPM/A) and the government of Unity State. In the last couple of years, Twic County of Warrap State was made an outlaw area. It was partly used by Gen. Stephen Buay after he tussled with the government and later upheld by Buay's nephew Gai Machiek who collaborated with their maternal uncles (Twic) to fight Ngok in exchange for being accommodated. Moreover, the government of South Sudan in person of South Sudan Defense Forces (SSPDF) unjustifiably sponsored Tit-weng (cattle camps and tribal armed youth) of Warrap State and promiscuously formed out of them what was wrongly named as Division (11), put in Mayom Anyuon. The primary intent of forming that army unit in Warrap State was to encounter the cattle raiders from Unity State. These forces and that of brigade 7A of Division (3) based in Mijak Kol had been devastatingly involved in the communal conflict between Ngok and Twic.

Nevertheless, some groups from Bul Nuer since 2013, chose to stay in Abyei, Aneet Area of Rumamer County in particular. The reasons for choosing Abyei were precisely economic and sociocultural. Some Ngok chieftaincies such as Diil and Achak have historical ties and blood lineages with some families in Bul and Alor Kur Kuot. However, Ngok of Abyei was envisaged by Nuer in general as one of Jieng's few sections which harbours no grudge of a political nature whatsoever against them. Members of Bul community were nicely treated by their brothers in Aneet, therefore quickly absorbed into Ngok community and were staying normally as residents not IDPs, particularly in Mabuony residential area adjacent to Mijak Kol. Many of them were doing lucrative businesses and became major suppliers of cattle.

As result, a class of business emerged, because the environment was conducive. In spite of some clashes which sporadically occurred between Bul-Nuer and Twic section of Kuac or sometimes between the latter and Alor Kur Kuot, Aneet continued to be a sanctum for all of them. Yet, some elements of Twic were trying to extend the differences between them and Nuer to Aneet, but Rumamer authorities, particularly late Hon. Mayot Kunit Miyan stood firmly against such malicious outlawry thinking. With this picture above, plot architects who were closely observing the dynamics on the ground, decided to use the local incubated mercenary of Gai Machiek and a militia camouflaged in Army uniform {Division 11} for the realisation of their long-thought-up ploy.

CHAPTER 12

A HENCHMAN WAS FOUND

*"A quidam often listens to anybody in his credulous search
for anything that could make him somebody."*

When operation of R-ARCISS kicked off, Twic County was taken by SPLM/A IO which appointed a politically unripe neophyte Deng Tong Goch Tong. SPLM IO is intrinsically an armed group which lacks effective tools for mobilisation and political organisation. In the aftermath, when its leaders returned to Juba for the implementation of R-ARCISS, many flocked in and could be typified in four main categories: job hunters which was the big group; supporters of ethnic politics; those engrafted by SPLM IG and other political interest groups such as JCE; and those discontent with Kiir's led SPLM faction policies. Analysing his political attitudes, Deng Tong falls into the first and third categories, it was not happenstantial for Deng Tong to be fervent that way on actualisation of Malwal Madut's scathing agenda against the people of Abyei.

Before Deng Tong Goch, Twic administration attempted during Atem Madut's governorship to expand its boundary by establishing illegal checkpoints in Athony and Mabuony within Abyei box, but Chief Administrator of the day, Kuol Alor Kuol sagaciously dealt with that truculence using UNISFA. However, circumstances were not on Twic's side to launch a wider scale offensive, the circle of intricacy completed in 2021 when intriguers finally found a suitable, inconsiderate amateur to implement their conspiracy. Deng Tong's political agenda in Twic had nothing to do with SPLM IO. He was shrewdly inset there through mentorship of his elders to execute their mission (Ngok Displacement from Southern Kiir Areas).

Instructed by his superiors in R-TNLA and the Council of States, Twic County's commissioner, Deng Tong Goch, unseemly to administrative norms, wrote a letter addressed to Abyei Area's Chief Administrator, Lt. Gen. Kuol Diem Kuol on 14 December 2021. Deng Tong requested from Abyei authorities to immediately cease land registry and survey in Aneet, Athony and what he intentionally misnamed as Majak Deng Muon. Deng Tong Goch executed word-for-word, his superior's instruction which he admitted in his statement to Aneet Facts Finding Committee. The Commissioner acknowledged that he conducted meetings with Twic national members of parliament and was officially asked to write to Hon. Chief Administrator on behalf of the group. Prior to meeting with Twic National Members of Parliament, he consulted with the First Vice-President in Juba and was advised not to solve the problem alone, but to involve others. SPLM/IO, particularly Dr. Riek Machar must be blamed here. He allowed the members of his party to be used as tools by Charles Majak Aleer and Majok Yak Majok of the SPLM/IG in Twic.

The political responsibility of Twic's members of parliament in influencing their Commissioner was undeniable as precisely stated in the Council of States report; *The committee found that honorable members of National Legislature representing Twic made incitement by influencing Hon. Eng. Deng Tong Goch, the commissioner of Twic County to write a direct letter to the Chief Administrator of Abyei in an insubordination to his superior, the Hon. Governor of Warrap State.* This instigation was also alluded to by Hon. Aleu Ayeny Aleu in his presentation before the Council of States on 3 March 2022, when he said that the letter written by Turalei County Commissioner was a *wanton provocation of the Abyei Administration and typical insubordination to the Governor of State.* (Attachment No.3)

The fact is that survey was done four years back in 2017, but in 2021, Abyei Administration was just opening the roads in Aneet residential area of Rumamer County. There was no survey in Athony Area of Alal County, nor elsewhere in Southern Kiir Counties. This generalisation and inclusion of other areas was done intentionally to comply with the whole stratagem, of claiming all Southern Kiir areas. Twic County's Commissioner claimed in his letter that Agok was given to Ngok internally displaced persons (IDPs) and were placed by Late Gen. James Yol Kuol Bol in 2002-2003 in the presence of then Governor of Bahar El Ghazal Mr.

Deng Alor Kuol. This claim was refuted by the Council of State's report in its finding No. (2):

> *"The Committee established that Agok area was there before 1997 as claimed by Twic community. That they gave it to Ngok through the request of late Dr. John Garang is not verifiable, simply because some say it was given to Ngok in 1994, 1997, 1998, 2002, 2003 and 2004. The conditions set out by Twic community to give out their land to Ngok as requested from them by Dr. John Garang are not traceable (no documentation); Internal Displaced Persons (IDPs) cannot be given land of more than 60 square kilometres, whatsoever the case."* (Attachment No. 3)

Twic County's Commissioner in the same letter, demanded from Abyei Administration to dismantle what he termed as an unofficial checkpoint in Athony and requested ASAA to disregard what he labelled as a community map (Abyei Box) which he allegedly said was intentionally created by people of Abyei to illegally annex Twic lands. He further requested Abyei Area's Authority to relocate three counties to Abyei town, which according to him were operating illegally South of Kiir River. (He was alluding to the administrations of Rumamer, Mijak and Alal Counties which are native homes for five Chiefdoms of Achak, Diil, Mareng, Manyuar, Anyiel and part of Abior in the South-West bordering Akoc-Thon}.

Deng Tong Goch also asked Abyei Administrative Area's

authority to direct the UN Forces in Abyei (UNISFA) to stop what he falsely described as incursion into Twic's lands. Twic County Commissioner's hyperbolic claims were mere instructions from his superiors who non-objectively doubted the legality of Abyei box. Yet, all their political and mental droppings were rubbished and refuted by the Council of States' Ad hoc Committee as detailed below:

> *"The Ad hoc Committee established that the objections made by the Hon. Members of the National Legislature representing Warrap State, Twic County, on Abyei box that it was drawn by NGOs is not true, because Abyei box was drawn by The Hague Arbitration and the ruling was highly welcomed by the government of Southern Sudan and Sudan. Therefore, the claim made by the members of National Legislature representing Twic County on the speech of the president in the governor's forum which they have mentioned in their letter is totally contrary to the Presidential order No.03/2015 for the establishment of Abyei Special Administrative Area, in the box. The Committee found out that the boundary line is not running inside River Kiir as claimed by Twic, but runs parallel to River Kiir at far south in the periodic swampy area of Alaal as it is in July 1955 and 1/1/1956 maps."*

The Committee established that the Presidential order No.03/2015 on the establishment of Abyei Special Administrative

Area, its four counties and Abyei municipality was based on the Abyei box. The Committee found out that the reception in honour of the visit of Dr. John Garang, Gen. Salva Kiir, Dr. Riek Machar, Dr. Lam Akol, Gen. Kuol Manyang Juuk etc to Agok area, was organised by Ngok not Twic. Twelve bulls were slaughtered. These twelve signified the following: nine for nine Ngok Chiefdoms; one bull for the visitors; one bull for Abyei; and one bull for Abiemnom IDPs hosted in Agok by Ngok. Furthermore, Gen. Aleu Ayeny Aleu, Governor of Warrap State admitted to Council of State's Adhoc Committee that he was misled when entering Agok with his gubernatorial flag flying He thereafter apologised to Hon. Chief Administrator of Abyei Special Administrative Area. (Attachment No. 3)

A most provocative and intrusive letter was written on 3 February 2022, by some ludicrous members of National Legislature (war-hawks), addressed to Abyei Area's Chief Administrator. This letter was in fact the source of the unfounded claims which were repeated by Twic County's Commissioner Deng Tong Goch in his letter to Lt. Gen. Kuol Diem Kuol, the ASAA's Chief Administrator. These MPs signed the petition and superciliously copied all the high tables including the Presidency. I wholeheartedly salute the few respected, real honorable members, Mama Adhardit Arop, Yolanda Awel Deng, Ayen Luka Ngor, Albino Mathem Ayuel, Rose Adau Deng and Joseph Malek Arop who refused to sign that reprehensible document which needlessly caused inveterate wounds and disfigured the relations between Ngok and Twic that resulted in loss of precious souls from both sides.

On the other hand, history must be recorded without prejudice, hence, everything should be exactly portrayed as everyone sees it. Below are the names of misleaders disguised as politicians who signed the script of death; Charles Majak Aleer, Majok Yak Majok, Angier Ring, Nyandeng Malek Dielic, Ajuet Moun Mawiir Rehan, Mangok Gum Nyuol, Kuany Mayom Deng, Elizabeth Acuei Yol, Mayom Kuoc Malek, Nyandeng Kerubino Kuanyin, Chan Malual Chan, Goc Makuac Mayol and Kuot Akec Thokluoi. These concealed bamboozlers should be dishonored, their crooked political attitudes be depicted exactly as they were, in order for younger generations to know the very persons who intricated that unnecessary calamity. I am quite sure, many noble men, women and real intellectuals in Twic and Warrap as a whole were averse to this insanity, but were overwhelmed by the influence of those aggravators hidden behind Bona Malwal Madut who did negatively influence Salva Kiir Mayardit. However, reigns are mortal like humans, history tells us how strong emperors and empresses, kings and despotic leaders lived and were finally taken. Power never lasts forever.

As mentioned earlier, there is no intrinsic difference between the letter written by Twic National Politicians and that of the Commissioner, Deng Tong Goch, the latter was just a reechoing of the other. Below is part of their dissonant claims:

"We the undersigned persons are members of Transitional National Legislature, who are very much concerned over continuous force occupation of Twic lands before and currently under your administrative management...
The borders you claimed as coming from The Hague

are strange and not known to Warrap, and Twic people
who are the actual owners of the lands.... Twic County
is not a party to the Abyei Arbitration because they were
not there in The Hague Court of Arbitration.

Abyei is part of former Kordufan Province now
known as Southern Kordufan Province and any talks of
borders between South Sudan and Sudan are governed
by borders of 1st January 1956.

The issue of Abyei Box is your own drawn up maps
with friendly NGOs we know, Such self-drawn up maps
as remarked by H.E the President of the Republic in the
Governor's conference that such maps drawn by NGOs."
(Attachment No.1)

With this ignoramus utterance above, the undersigned
misleaders did expose their riffraffish political shallowness in an
unprecedented manner. Those parroters, to wit, Charles Majak
Aleer and Majok Yak Majok were too subjective and politically
malaised with Bonaism. *(Bona syndrome, is kind of political sadism*
characterised by unquenchable compulsion for seeing Ngok people of
Abyei estranged and persecuted).

Most anti-Ngok politicians in Twic were naively confusing
two different factors; the unresolved political status of Abyei
between Sudan and South Sudan; and Ngok historical rights in
their ancestral region. Yes, Abyei is one of the unfinished political
businesses between CPA's parties, now the sovereign Republics of
South Sudan and Sudan, but that cannot turn it (Abyei) *nullius*
in bonis. However, and according to article (1.3, a & b) of the

Agreement on the Resolution of Abyei Conflict (Abyei Protocol), people of Abyei are entitled to vote on a referendum to choose between; Abyei retains its special administrative status in the north; or returns to Bahar el Ghazl in the South.

Lamentably, Ngok was denied that right until Southern Sudan gained independence, and as I mentioned in the previous chapters, Abyei region was left in the lurch in a state of quasi-statelessness which is not sovereignly Sudan nor South Sudan. Even though people of Abyei had unequivocally declared their position six decades ago when they joined the struggle side by side with the people of Southern Sudan, again proclaimed it in Agok Conference in 2003, and finally in October 2013 when they unilaterally conducted their referendum. Regrettably, Kiir's led government failed to recognise the outcome of the referendum in which people of Abyei overwhelmingly voted for joining South Sudan. However, being in this state cannot dismiss the existence of Ngok Dinka of Abyei and the fact that they had been inhabiting Abyei area for ages.

The parties to the Comprehensive Peace Agreement went to The Hague for Arbitration, but the border redefined by the Court was the northern boundary between Abyei and Kordofan. The Southern border was known as it stood on January 1, 1956 between the then provinces of Kordofan and Bahar el Ghazal. It should be made clear that The Hague tribunal had nothing to do with Twic-Ngok boundaries (Abyei protocol article:1.4). Furthermore, neighbouring communities to Ngok including Twic were represented in the delegation which went to The Hague as witnesses so denying Abyei Box because Twic was not officially a party to the tribunal. But this was a hoax created by Bona Malwal and his political auxiliaries.

Amidst this high degree of confusion and disinformation made by Bona Malwal's political henchmen in Twic, people may wrongly think that Ngok Dinka of Abyei were physically carried off from their native home to Kordofan Province. To shed light on this issue, below are writings of some British Governors of Kordofan:

Ngok did not ask for or receive refuge from the Humr. They did not physically move from one area to another. What occurred in 1905 was that because of Dinka complaints about Humr raids, the British authorities decided to transfer the Ngok and part of Twic Dinka from the administrative control of Bahar el Ghazl Province to Kordofan Province. This action put the Ngok and the Humr under the authority of the same governor. Michael Tibbs, the last British District Commissioner for Dar Misseriya, has said that in 1952, when the Ngok became a part of the District Council, joining into it with the Misseriya, they were not members of the Misseriya tribe, did not come under the jurisdiction of the Misseriya leadership, and had their own court. [52]

The record shows that the Ngok were administered separately. For example, in 1908 in the list of tributes paid to Kordofan Province, the Dinka are included separately from the Arabs. There were separate entries for the Ngok in the 1932 Kordofan budget, which also showed the Ngok paying taxes directly to the Kordofan government, not through the Humr Nazier. Misseriya tax lists from the late 1940s do not list the Ngok. The evidence from the

---

52   Abyei boundaries commission report

Condominium records is conclusive that the Ngok Dinka courts were independent of the Misseriya courts and were administered separately throughout the period of the Condominium. Chief Kwol Arop's Court functioned informally throughout the 1920s, until it was designated Court Number 12 (separate from Misseriya courts) in 1936. In that year outgoing District Commissioner J.W. Robertson described a separate Court system for the Humr and the Ngok. Of the latter, he wrote: *The Dinka Court is a flourishing Concern*... At the end of the Condominium in 1954 Michael Tibbs recorded that the Ngok continued to have their own court.

It is not Abyei alone that was affected by these distortive administrative orders which created the border dispute between the North and South, below is another example of a territorial manipulative transfer. Several border shifts and territorial transfers similar to the one involving Abyei took place between the north and south and sowed the seeds of many border disputes currently hindering cordial relations between the two Sudans. This process of boundary changes reached a climax in 1922 when colonial officials forcibly evicted the entire population of the Kafka Kinga enclave in an attempt to create a *tangible division between 'Arab' and 'African' groups along the border zone between Darfur and Baher Al Ghazal* The region which had previously been a melting pot of cultures, became an impenetrable barrier. In 1958 the military regime of General Ibrahim Abboud annexed the Kafia Kingi enclave to Darfur.[53]

---

53   Dr. Kweisi sanseulotte Greendige, *Abyei from A shared past to a Contested future*, May 2011

A similar transfer occurred in 1924 when the Munroe Wheatley Agreement changed the border between the Reziegat of Darfur and the Malwal Dinka of Bahar al Ghazl. The boundary between the two communities and the provinces they inhabited previously lay at the bank of the River Kiir known in the north as the Bahar al Arab. However, the agreement shifted the boundary 14 miles, or 22 km, south of the river. The agreement was designed to allow the Reziegat, who the British were attempting to woo as allies, greater access to the rich grazing lands just south of the river and reduce conflict between them and the Malwal Dinka who inhabited the area. This border shift was implemented without the authorisation of the Governor General in Khartoum and without consulting the Dinka at the time. As a result, the agreement is currently contested by the GoSS.

Bona's political devotees in Twic, who irksomely masticated his saying, *Abyei is Kordofan,* should have understood that what happened in 1905, was a mere administrative order. Abyei was re-districted under Kordofan and no popular consultation was made, exactly like what transpired in 2015, when Raja County of Western Bahar el Ghazal State was amalgamated with Awiel West and Awiel North Counties of Northern Bahar el Ghazal and renamed as Lol State. The difference between this case of Raja and Abyei is that the latter was transferred from one region to another which now fractured into two Republics of South Sudan and Sudan, while Raja, Awiel North and Awiel West are from the same region. Bona's political acolytes were implausibly driven by hatred, hence debunked themselves in an ignoble manner. Imagine asking Abyei Area's Chief Administrator to relocate UNISFA'S forces deployed at South-Kiir back to their HQs in Abyei Town! This signifies how ignorant they were and that they did not understand the simple rules which normally guide such situations. Those of Charles Majak Aleer and Majok Yak Majok envisaged UNISFA as freebooters hired by Ngok and placed under Chief Administrator's command!

Shortly before the independence of Southern Sudan, Abyei was invaded by Sudan's Armed Forces, but Troika, African Union, through its AUHIP exerted more effort to bring the parties on board. As a result, the government of Sudan and Sudan People's Liberation Movement under the auspices of Ethiopian Prime Minister Males Zenawi signed an agreement on 20 June 2011. The parties to the Temporary Administrative and Security Arrangements Accord asked the United Nations to assist in maintaining the security in Abyei Area. Hence, Security Council at its (6567) meeting adopted the resolution No.1990 (2011), recognising that the situation in Abyei demands an urgent response because it constitutes a threat to international peace and security.

Below are some of the articles that represent UNISFA's core mandate in Abyei;

1. Decides to establish, for a period of six months, the United Nations Interim Security Force for Abyei (UNISFA), taking into account the Agreement between the Government of Sudan and the Sudan People's Liberation Movement on Temporary Arrangements for the Administration and Security of the Abyei Area, and further decides that UNISFA shall comprise of a maximum of 4,200 military personnel, 50 police personnel, and appropriate civilian support;

2. Decides that UNISFA shall have the following mandate:

    a. Monitor and verify the redeployment of any Sudan Armed Forces, Sudan People's Liberation Army or its successor, from the Abyei Area as defined by the Permanent Court of Arbitration; henceforth, the Abyei Area shall be demilitarised from any forces other than UNISFA and the Abyei Police Service;

3. Acting under Chapter V11 of the Charter of the United Nations, authorizes UNISFA within its capacities and its area of deployment to take the necessary actions to:

    a. without prejudice to the responsibilities of the relevant authorities, to protect civilians in the Abyei Area under imminent threat of physical violence,

    b. protect the Abyei Area from incursion by unauthorized elements, as defined in the Agreement, and

    c. ensure security in the Abyei Area. [54]

The area defined by the Permanent Court of Arbitration mentioned above in article (2,a) is what is now popularly known as Abyei Box and the unauthorised elements in article (3,b) could be state actors like the illegal existence of SAF masked as oilfield police, Thomas Thiel's soldiers of fortune in the north and the illegal deployment of SSPDF in Agok and Athony following Ngok-Twic Conflict, or non-state actors such as tribal militias or any armed desperados.

This was how UNISFA came to exist in Abyei, it was a triadic

---

54   United Nations Security Council's Resolution No.1990/2011

agreement between Republic of Sudan, Sudan People's Liberation Movement, now the Republic of South Sudan and United Nations. What deuteragonists were trying to achieve was to make Southern Kiir Areas be envisaged as disputed between Ngok and Twic, hence helplessly echoing their father-figure's groundless canard. All those unsubstantiated demands were refuted by South Sudan Council of States' Ad-hoc Committee. What some Twic political prank-sters don't comprehend clearly is that their unseemly attempt at denying the legality of Abyei Box and the inviolability status of Abyei's Southern border as stood in January 1,1956, is tantamount to undermining the legitimacy of the entire boundaries between Sudan and South Sudan!

Politicians should be inquisitive researchers. If Twic County's Members of National Legislature read with scrutiny, the Abyei protocol, Abyei Boundaries Commission report and PCA ruling, they could have understood the fact that the southern border of Abyei Area has no linkage with PCA's ruling.

Since the Malakal conference organised by Southern Front in 1964, and the round table in the following year, Southern Sudan was defined as the provincial boundaries of Bahar el Ghazl, Equatoria and Upper Nile as stood on January 1, 1956. As Southern Front's Secretary-General, Bona's role was operative in both political activities, ergo, Abyei was elided from that defi-nition. However, Machakos Agreement and Abyei Protocol were principally based on the same definition, therefore, it's imperative for young Bonaers to understand. It would be political duplicity to use January 1, 1956 for ceding Abyei to northern Sudan and again deny to illegally grabbing some parts of it! It is clearly stated in

Abyei Protocol article 1.4 that *The January 1, 1956 line between the north and south will be inviolate...* This inviolability status of Abyei's southern borders shall continue until the final status is achieved.

CHAPTER 13

ATTACKS ON ANEET

"The day myopic politicians succeeded in spoiling the peaceful neighourliness between Twic and Ngok, I considered the adage that says; politics is a dirty game."

It is not unprecedented for neighbors to dispute over a piece of land, that happens even between members of one community, but there are traditional mechanisms for resolving such matters according to the norms of that very community. I am quite sure that Ngok of Abyei and Twic of Warrap State know their exact borders. They can amicably resolve the matter, if freshly seated under trees away from cytotoxic environment of politicians. Nowhere, does everyone neighbour everyone, because there are always inlands and frontiers. It is not the whole Abyei area that borders the whole Twic County, there are only eight subsections at the border, four from each side. Ngok community comprises of nine chieftaincies as follows; Bongo, Alie, Achueing, Achak, Mareng, Abior, Anyiel, Mannyuar and Diil. The Chiefdoms which have a border with Twic are the latter four chieftaincies of Abior, Anyiel, Mannyuar and Diil and the four sections of Twic are Kuac Anganya, Amol, Adiang and Akoc-thon. According to ensnarement drawn by hoaxsters, Kuac Anganya, subsection of Amol, namely the family of Teeng Akuei, was assigned to kindle the fight. However, and according to Chief Bagat Makuac Abiem who made the presentation before Aneet's Facts Finding Committee on behalf of Ngok Dinka's chiefs, the problem started earlier in the form of episodical recurrences:

In 2005 the differences started on the collection of revenues. Capt. Deng Monynuer Kuol (Jokrial), Magir Malual, Agueet Monyluak Minyang Agueet and three others from Ngok were killed. The case was investigated by SPLA headquarters but remained unresolved.

In 2016 during the reign of CA Chol Deng Alak and Bona Banek Biar, who was the Governor of Warrap State, a conference was organised in Ajak Kuac and attended by the Chiefs, in the house of Bol Ahol. In the said meeting, it was claimed that the Twic community raised the need for the Ngok to relocate to the north of River Kiir as they were residing in Twic areas. The Commissioners informed the gathering that the issue of the border is a prerogative of President Kiir.

In 2017 an illegal checkpoint was established in the areas bordering Aneet during the governorship of Kon Manyiel. At the checkpoint people were taxed, harassed and threatened.

In 2018, Arop Atak killed two boys, the son and a nephew of Chief Akonon Ajuong Deng in Tong-liet, He was arrested but later set free without accountability.[55]

In 2019, Sultan Teeng Deng Teeng, Chief of Anganya, mobilised the youth to remove the signposts and demolished the Payam office in Mading-Jokthiang in the southwest of Agok. Sultan Teeng Deng Teeng came again in May 2021 with some Chiefs: Mayen Kur Mayen, Deng Kol Ajal, Ring Wol Chan, Yak Aguek and slaughtered a bull in Mading-Jokthiang in the house of Deng Changath and claimed that area belonged to them. Commissioner of Rumamer County arrested Sultan Deng Teeng for attempting to slaughter another bull in Aneet. As a result, violence erupted and subsequently some youth from Twic raped a number of women in Mading-Jokthiang who were hospitalised in MSF hospital in Juljok., Unfortunately, no one was arrested.

On 9 February 2022, Twic Chiefs and youth entered Mading-Jokthiang, beat some people up and arbitrarily arrested them. On 10 February 2022, two cars entered Aneet Market with one vehicle mounted with 12.7 artillery and shot at people in the market. Four people were killed and three were injured. It was claimed that one of the vehicles belonged to a businessman Bol Ahol Ngor. This was also confirmed by the Council of States Ad hoc Committee's report. A businessman called Bol Ahol had contributed his personal pickup mounted with a 12.7 millimetre to Twic youth to fight against Ngok.

---

55   Chief Bagat Makuac Abiem's representation before the Facts Finding Committee

Forces from Mayom Anyuon, the HQs of Division 11 were said to have been moved on 11 February 2022, after they slaughtered two bulls. They came with four vehicles at night from four directions: Mabuony, Juoljok, Ajak-Thony and one car was directed to Rumkoor in case of any reinforcement from there. This matched with the statement of Abyei Acting Commissioner of Police, Brig. Gen. Ring Mawien Nyikuach;

> *The forces in Mayom Anyuon were released and given bullets leaving Mijak-Kol under the leadership of Chom Ring. The forces proceeded to Agok and began their attack from Mading-Jokthiang, Mabuony, Aneet and Juoljok. These forces attacked people, burned houses, looted and abducted children in Mabuony and many were killed, all these atrocities were recorded by UNISFA.*

In his statement to Aneet's Facts Finding Committee, Abyei Area's Chief Administrator, Lt. Gen. Kuol Diem Kuol dubbed what happened as fighting triggered by some elements from eastern Twic. Gen. Kuol affirmed that Abyei maps endorsed by the government of South Sudan were based on 1/1/1956 boundary of Bahar el Ghazl and Kordofan. He bolstered his statement by saying that Abyei Box was drawn by The Hague Tribunal Arbitration of 2009. Therefore, Agok and Akur are part of Abyei. According to Hon. Chief Administrator, the root causes of the conflict are clear and include:

1. Incitement of Twic by some politicians in Juba. Highlighted in four letters

2. Poverty which has affected much of Northern Bahar el Ghazal sub region
3. Challenges of command in the Army
4. Boundary dispute. [56]

The attack resulted in the following losses: Eighty-five people were killed. Seventy-one houses were burned in different places. The Chief Administrator reaffirmed that there were no attacks instigated by Ngok community against Twic He regrettably said:

> *"This is a war of shame. Victory in such a war is not victory."*

Furthermore, the Paramount Chief of Ngok Dinka of Abyei, Bulabek Deng Kuol was interviewed by AFFC on 25 March 2022, and he stated the following: Aneet belongs to Diil Community, and it is particularly a land of Payath, Pajook, and Pabuk-Jaak sub-clans. The relationship between the Ngok and Twic communities has always been smooth. They have always worked together in the issue of the movement across the border, as non-Ngok Dinka always required a pass permit from Sultan Deng Majok to move their animals north of Abyei. Twic herders would make their stop near Nyin-Deng Ayuel by the river (Alaal) and Ngok would take it from there heading north. They worked as partners and allies. The most recent example is during the conflict between Aguok and

---

56   Lt. Gen. Kuol Diem Kuol's report before the Facts Finding Committee

Apuk, most people from those communities were accommodated by the Ngok community. The Paramount Chief emphasised that no sons of Ngok went to Twic to burn or attack their villages. He reaffirmed that Ngok and Twic are socially related, and even if a Ngok kills a person from Twic, some families from Ngok will cry too.[57]

Aneet Market after the February 2022 attack

---

57   Paramount Chief Bulabek Deng Kuol's statement before the Facts Finding Committee

CHAPTER 14

WAS HUSSEIN
SUITED TO THE MISSION?

Two weeks after the conflict erupted in Aneet, South Sudan's president, Salva Kiir Mayardit issued a republican order on 24 February 2022 (No.05/2022) for the formation of an investigation committee to look into the inter-communal clashes that broke out on 10 February 2022 in Aneet. Without prior consultation, Kiir handpicked one of his aides, Hussein Abdel Bagi whom he assigned to a service delivery cluster in the presidency. This move raised skepticism, because the nature of that mission (conflict between Ngok and Twic) was a politically motivated matter relating to administration and governance. So Dr. Riek Machar Teny was the felicitous figure among those in the presidency to lead that Facts Finding Committee. Apart from his meritocracy, he was the head of Southern Sudan's delegation to The Hague when parties to the Comprehensive Peace Agreement sought international arbitration on Abyei. These community feuds require eminent personalities such as Prof. Moses Machar Kachual, Hon. George Kongor Arop, Hon. Angelo Beda or anyone whose impartiality would be unquestionable by the disputants. *Hussein Abdel Bagi is just a mediocre person who lacks experience and moral ethos to lead a mission of such a composite nature.*

AFFC's work stumbled first when the office of the president used "Settlement" for Aneet instead of Area or Town. According to the people of Abyei, the term was pre-emptive and there was no exonerative explanation given for choosing it. However, Abyei Community in Juba put its protest in written form urging the committee to use a neutral term as quoted below;

> *"Your Excellency, in relation to the above-cited Order, our different Ngok Dinka Community bodies met and asked us, the undersigned community leaders, to bring to your notice the following critical observations and suggest solutions as follows:*
>
> *1. The reference to Aneet Settlement is of great concern to us and needs to be corrected to read Aneet Town, as use of the word Settlement prematurely affirms Twic's unfounded claim that they offered the area to settle Ngok Dinka Internally Displaced*
> *2. That the inclusion of Hon Charles Majak Aleer and Hon Nyandeng Malek Delic in the Committee membership affects the objectives and neutrality of the*

Committee, as the two honorable members are on record as perpetrators, among others, of the events that led to the repeated attacks on Aneet Town since February 10th

3. To cement the neutrality of the Committee, it is Ngok's Dinka Community's view that members hailing from Ngok and Twic communities be excluded from the membership of the Committee

4. Finally, as this is an investigation or fact-finding Committee, we suggest the inclusion of a senior representative of the National Ministry of Justice in the membership of the Committee." [58]

Unfortunately, these reservations fell on deaf ears and that was the beginning of dubiety. The AFFC met separately with Ngok and Twic communities in Juba, a move envisaged as an admittance that the conflict was initiated by Juba-based politicians. Moreover, two elders of Twic and Ngok, Hon. Bona Malwal Madut and Dr. Francis Mading Deng issued a joint statement asking the contending communities to hose down, unfortunately their call was not heeded.

A few days after fighting erupted, Gen. Akuei Ajou, Commander of the 3rd infantry Division in Northern Bahar el Gazl was sent to Aneet, despite the no militarisation status of Abyei Area according to United Nations Security Council's resolution1990. The move was welcomed, particularly by the most devastated people of Abyei.

---

58   Abyei Communities in Juba complaints to Facts Finding Committee

However, and according to Abyei Acting Commissioner of Police; forces were first deployed at Mading-Jokthiang and Maker Banydit which was said to have improved the situation. Brig. Gen. Ring Mawien Nyikuach blamed Gen. Akuei for deploying away the forces from Aneet which resulted in the attacks of March the 5th 2022. Many SSPDF personnel from Twic who were deployed in Abyei Independent Brigade (AIB) were said to have defected and joined their communities in the fight. As I mentioned earlier, formation of Division 11 based in Mayom Anyuon was unprofessional, a tribal, promiscuous armed youth cannot overnight turn into a well-disciplined army!

Ngok community was in a real stupefaction, unable to internalise the matter, and after the extensive attacks continued, the situation turned critical and more than fifty thousand people fled from Aneet and its surrounding areas to Abyei town. Furthermore, Misseriya attacked Abyei after infiltrating up to Mading-Thon on the western bank of Nyamuora stream. Residents of Gongbial, Abyei-Thony, and Duop were at a shooting range, so they quickly ran towards the eastern part of Abyei and assembled at UNISFA's gate expecting protection.

Unfortunately, these dispirited people who were attacked back and forth were denied entry by UNISFA. Mading-Thon battle marked a turning point for Ngok, after they realised there was no other option than to withstand and face that existential threat. Some called it *Tong Piny Ce Guud/ a fight of no choice*, a metaphor implying the inescapability of that figh. Hence, youth voluntarily flocked together, mostly teenagers and primary school pupils as a response to that unskippable call. I still remember how they looked exhausted and wild when I visited them in Juljok school in Agok, where they were assembling and vowed not to leave their home behind. This was how Tiit-Bai or Home Guards came about, but hitherto, it was still unnamed.

Other than direct attacks on the ground, cyberactive warniks opened another front. Multiple incendiary pages appeared and were malevolently used for political mobilisation and character vilification. Some of those pages were, Twic Nhom Detam, Wunrok TV and Ajak-Kuac TV. Hateful messages were circulated online on those pages and that has arguably extended the fight. Overseas warmongers have also joined the incitement through live videos using disparaging speeches as tools for nurturing hatred in youth to continue the fight. In this respect, Mayar Cier Deng Thiepdok, Aguer Brach and Deng Dut Koor were leading that diabolical campaign which would later be countered by Kuol Mathok Tong and one of Tiit-Bai's fighters disguised as Smart Dog. Subsequently, Ngok youth opened some pages to encounter that systemic disinformation.

Heretofore, Tiit -Bai were still maintaining their defensive position respecting elders' instructions to never cross what was believed to be the border between Ngok and Twic. Many attacks occurred, but Ngok youth never crossed the border until grans were horrendously massacred in Rumamer. Chief Lal Kon Tingloth, Kuol Nyok Wun-Aceng, Mayath Maluk and other elderly women, Alek Makuei Deng Leng, Awai Magak and others. Ngok's youth were seriously provoked by the way elders were cold-bloodedly butchered, therefore shifted it a little bit from defense to pursuance.

However, Twic established a global machinery for propaganda, the objective of that political illusionism was to delude the public, particularly the people of Equatoria and Upper Nile who they knew may have no better understanding of the nature of the strife between Ngok and Twic. To conceal their sordid acts, Twic politicians' agents aimed at sullying the image of Ngok public figures. Chief Administrator of the day, Lt. Gen. Kuol Diem Kuol was one of their main targets, many lies were trumped up displaying him as commander of a fanciful force phonily named Adichol Battalion. Under that pressure, Gen. Kuol Diem was not able to visit Aneet, and sent his aides, Gen. Chol Thouc Chol, Hon. Kilek Kon and Hon. Mayot Kuniet Miyen. The CA managed to visit Agok when he was officially receiving a delegation of Abyei National Parliamentary Caucus which was visiting the area to solace their distressed community.

Abyei members of National Legislature – R-TNLA and Council of States were the first to react by releasing a condemnation statement calling for the two sisterly communities of Twic and Ngok to cease violence. Conversely, Twic MPs were very much cognisant with their political cozenage. As the conflict's actual fanners, they did not bother to issue any call for bloodshed terminus. Due to logistical challenges, Abyei Parliamentary Caucus's mission delayed until a good Samaritan chartered a plane. On 19 February 2022, a delegation comprised of six members of National Legislature and a member of (AJOC) arrived at Agok airstrip. They were welcomed to the ACAD premises and summarily briefed on the situation. After briefing, CA took the delegation to conflict-affected sites in Aneet and Juoljok markets which had been burned by perpetrators. On the way to Abyei Town, the delegation stopped briefly at Abathok Area of Mijak County where a market was partially burned on 16 February 2022.[59]

The delegation conducted a series of meetings with the cabinet and Abyei Area's Legislative Council and was elaborately briefed by the Chief Administrator. In the following day, members of the caucus met separately with Chiefs, youth and women's groups. On the fourth day, the delegation visited Abathok where attackers from Twic County looted some cattle and burned a child in a hut, then proceeded to meet government officials in Agok. From there, the delegation divided into two, some visited the boys (TB) in Juoljok, and others went to the army garrison in Mijak Kol. On the same day, the delegation returned to Abyei and conducted its last meeting with UNISFA. After returning to Juba, Abyei's representatives in the council of states made a lobby, hence, Gen. Aleu Ayeny Aleu, Governor of Warrap State and Lt. Gen. Kuol Diem Kuol, the Chief Administrator of Abyei Area were summoned by the Council of States in March 2022.[60]

In Juba, leaders of the two communities were convoked before AFFC's board departed to Warrap State and proceeded to Twic County where a series of meetings was conducted, first with Warrap State's Governor, Gen. Aleu Ayeny Aleu, Twic County's Commissioner and interest groups of Chiefs, women and youth.

---

59   Delegation of Abyei National Parliamentary Caucus visited Abyei on 19 February 2022/ led by Hon. Asha Abbas, Tabitha Chol Minyel, Margaret Vito Akuar, Teresa Chol Aguek, Chabour Goch Alie, Jok Alor Bulabek and a member of Abyei Joint Oversight Committee, Nyankuac Ngor

60   Ibid

The committee admitted to facing many challenges in collecting information from interviewees and I quote;

> *"The Committee encountered difficulty while gathering data in the field where respondents intentionally avoided surrendering or providing objective answers. Often biased information was presented to the committee and it had to verify it accordingly as individuals identified with their communities and could hardly be impartial."*

In Abyei, AFFC conducted the same who-shot-John-like investigations and met with Chief Administrator, Commissioner of Rumamer, Acting Commissioner of Police Chiefs and other interest groups of women and youth. After discussions were concluded in Abyei, the committee headed to Majak-Kol Barracks which was envisaged as a neutral and secure site for signing the Cessation of Hostilities Agreement. However, SSPDF forces of Division Three and the bodyguards of Twic County's Commissioner had a disagreement which threatened the safety of the delegation as forces came to a standoff.

With that inconvenience, a chance for signing a document was hampered, hence rescheduled to be organised in Awiel under the aegis of Hon. Tong Akeen Ngor, Governor of Northern Bahar el Ghazal State. AFFC's members employed their influences to bring the contending parties together, though Twic's Chiefs were highly pressured by their sons at the national level to accept no deal at that particular time. Bona's misled devotees, even though the right was not on their side, believed they had enough might, hence, they aimed at occupying Southern Kiir areas first before signing any deal.

However, AFFC continued its pressure on the chiefs of both sides until they signed an agreement on Cessation of Hostilities on 4 April 2022 as mentioned below;

> *"Without any reservations, the two communities have decided willingly and agreed to the terms as ways to immediately address the current conflict:*
>
> 1. *To declare immediate cessation of hostilities and to stop all forms of aggression whether direct or indirect between the two communities;*
> 2. *Rejuvenate peaceful coexistence and social cohesion between the two communities and to ensure trust and confidence;*
> 3. *End all forms of direct or indirect provocations whether verbal or written including hate speeches on the social media and other medium of communications;*
> 4. *Stop all forms of unauthorized roadblocks or check points;*
> 5. *Ensure free movement of people and goods in respective areas of jurisdiction including in Aneet and surrounding areas;*
> 6. *Allow the National Government without any reservations to convene and facilitate peace and reconciliation dialogue which should establish the root causes of the conflict with the objective of finding*

permanent solution to the conflict between the two communities;

7. *Recognise the fact that interstate boundaries are responsibilities of the national government, not states or communities;*

8. *Ensure that all accused persons from either side must face justice according to the laws of South Sudan;*

9. *Ensure our commitment to peace and stability, we are determined to accept the outcome of the permanent peace settlement that should convene at the place of the National Government's choice;*

10. *Immediately suspend without any reservations all forms of survey in Aneet/Agok or surrounding areas until such further notice from the National Government;*

11. *Reiterate our role as chiefs and local authorities, we are determined to help ensure proper security and peace in all areas of our jurisdiction;*

12. *Henceforth, in the event of any attack on either side, the Chief from the attackers will be fully held to account."* [61]

The Agreement was witnessed by Hon. Joseph Monytueil, Governor of Unity State and Deputy Chairperson of Aneet Facts Finding Committee, Hon. Tong Akeen Ngor, Governor of

---

61   Cessation of Hostilities Agreement Between Twic and Ngok Communities/Northern Bahar el Gazal/ Awiel/ April 2022

Northern Bahar el Ghazl State and Hon. Dhieu Mathok Diing Wol, Secretary of the Committee. However, the aspired peace was achieved only in papers, but sentiment and general mood of the two communities remained antipathetic. Shortly after parties signed the CoHA, Twic's youth ambushed a vehicle heading to Abyei from Wau, passengers were harassed and a lad named Deng Kuol Dupier was taken hostage and finally killed after kidnappers manipulatively took ransom from his family. Such a nasty act is alien to our South Sudanese norms. Deng Kuol Dupier's killing was a clear violation to article (1& 5) and served as a unilateral abolishment of the CoHA. The Cessation of Hostilities Agreement was entirely nullified by Twic and Hussein's committee proved to be an ineffective instrument. It failed to condemn the killings, let alone take action against the perpetrators.

Upon return to Juba, VP Hussein Abdel Bagi whetted his teeth and unjustifiably decided to detain many Abyei Area's constitutional post holders, army, police officers, noncommissioned officers and some civilians without due legal procedures. On April1, 2022, Hussein summoned the following SSPDF officers from Abyei to Juba: Maj. Gen. Kuol Monyluak Dak, the Commander of Abyei Independent Brigade (AIB); Brig. Gen. Deng Bol Athuai; Col. Ayuel Kiir Chol; and Lt. Col. Bagat Malual Bagat. These high-ranked officers were just detained upon arrival at Juba international airport by the Military Intelligence (MI). On 5 May 2022, and 20 May respectively, Brig. Gen. Police, Ring Mawien Nyikuach and Brig. Gen. Anyiel Agon Arop were also summoned and detained. Moreover, four ASAA's constitutional post holders were also summoned and arbitrarily detained on 16 May

2022, their names were Hon. Mayot Kuniet Miyen, Minister for Physical Infrastructure and Public Utilities; Hon. Chol Pur Chol, Commissioner of Rumamer County and Hon. Akuei Akoon Wel, Commissioner of Alal County.

Many observers believe that the arbitrary detention was influenced by Twic politicians who naively thought that those officers were participating in the conflict. Surprisingly, the situation worsened and conflict escalated after their detention. Abyei community unapologetically accused AFFC's members and Hussein Abdel Bagi in particular of being biased to Twic. No justification whatsoever for Hussein to detain this number of Ngok's officials while actual provocateurs were swaggeringly and freely moving with him! The Agreement on Cessation of Hostilities was unfortunately a stillbirth, none of its provisions was implemented, nor underminers held accountable.

Despite the severity of the flooding, Twic youth, renegade elements from SSPDF Division 11 (Mayom Anyuon) together with Gai Machiek's mercenaries pervasively attacked Abyei areas hither and thither during the rainy season, but Ngok Home Guards (Tiit-Bai) continued their deterrence and pursuit strategy. Attackers were chased up to where they had come from and this was how some Twic hamlets got ravaged. Areas of Rey-Ayan, Tong-Liet, Anyiel -Kuac, Manh-Awan and other thorps at the borderline up to Ajak-Kuac were destabilised and partially de-peopled.

Committee's Secretariat, March 2022

*Hon. Aleu Ayieny Aleu, Governor of Warrap State (R) and Hon.
Kuol Deim Kuol, Chie Administrator of ASAA (L) signing CoHA
in Aweil - NBGs.*

Committee's Secretariat March 2022

Picture showing Paramount Chief of Ngok Bulabek Kuol Deng (L) and Ag. Paramount Chief of Twic Deng Mayen Deng (R) signing CoHA in Aweil-NBGs.

Committee's Secretariat March 2022

H.E. Hussein Abdelbagi Akol, Vice-President of the Republic and Chairperson of the Ancet Inter-Commual Investigation Committee signing CoHA as a Guarantor in Aweil-NBGs

CHAPTER 15

THE SECOND WAVE
OF ATTACKS

In the month of September 2022, information kept coming that Twic was preparing for a destructive attack to sweep Ngok out from Agok Area and declare as its territory. Imagine! People from Twic community normally call their relatives in Abyei to stay vigilant. If this was not political bewitchery, Ngok and Twic could have not feuded at all. They are in fact one people, Kuac sections in particular. It is seldom to find a Ngok family that has no linkage with Twic, many fighters of Abyei Home Guard's (Tiit-Bai) mothers are from Twic, it was an anomalous situation where nephews preyed upon their uncles and vice versa.

On 10 October 2022, Agok was attacked from three directions, Gai Machiek's insurgents from southeast attacked Juoljok. Akuar, Kuac and Amol stimulated by some renegades from Division 11

(Mayom Anyuon) and Mijak Kol attacked Mabuony and Aneet, youth from Twic west came from the southwest and attacked Maker. The number of Tiit Bai in Agok was not enough, though they tried hard to face that triadic attack, but their ability for deterrence languished.

Roads were completely cut off by floods and that made reinforcement very hard and ineffective. Youth in Abyei Town moved since the wee hours upon receiving alerts from their peers in Agok. Reinforcers from the nearest areas of Abathok, Majbuong and Wunpeeth joined, yet failed to repulse the attackers. That ghastly attack necessitated a tactical withdrawal, but in the process, some sank in Achook River and others with the heart of a tiger refused to turn their backs and leave Aneet behind. In the meantime, when Tiit-Bai insurgents were regrouping and reorganising, attackers looted the few remnant shops in Aneet market. Furthermore, Twic's netizens were victoriously celebrating the capture of Agok and hurriedly sent the information to their shadowy cohorts at J1, who promptly airlifted forces from Tiger Division to Aneet.[62]

The situation was messy as some injured persons were still lying at Agok Airstrip, unexpectedly an aircraft landed while Tiit-Bai were doing some cleaning. Before touching down, a soldier chanted *Mayardit Oyee*, but Tiit-Bai waved Three Fingers which is a symbol of Ngok Atung-Diak. That soldier was said to have remained on board. Another soldier identified his in-law who was army personnel among dissidents beside Agok Airstrip.

It took SSPDF's GHQs nearly two weeks to claim that forces

---

62   Statement of Abyei Civil Societies Organization

were sent to restore security to the Area. This move came after Aneet's Facts Finding Committee issued a statement on the matter. However, many in Abyei believed that these forces were not directly dispatched by the Ministry of Defense, but it was a mission forged by elements in and around South Sudan's presidency. These forces, instead of proceeding to military barracks in Mijak Kol or Rum-koor, took Agok Administrative Unit as their base, others in the police station and some occupied schools and civilian houses.

It was a bewildering situation. How would these forces restore stability while dysfunctioning the work of the civil administrations in the area? The intention of deploying those forces according to observers was to depopulate Agok, militarise it and officially deal with as a disputed area. If their aims were to refixate the situation, forces should have been posted at the borderline between the two conflicting communities, not inside Agok! For many people in Abyei, SSPDF's involvement in Aneet was a byword for occupation, which they likened to exactly what Sudan had been doing in the northern part of Abyei (SAF presence at Kec/Diffra disguised as oil police). Vice President and the Chairperson of Aneet Facts Finding Committee Hussein Abdel Bagi had been quoted on many occasions declaring that Aneet was the final destination for the forces. This contradicts the government's official narrative and conforms with Ngok's conjecture.

Following the illegal deployment of SSPDF's Tiger forces in Agok, southern part of Abyei Area turned into a den of hoodlums. Armed groups were committing crimes hither and yon with impunity, Twic and Gai Machiek's insurgents in particular. Tiit- Bai was the only force for deterrence after UNISFA's failure to execute its core mandate which is prevention of unauthorised armed groups from incursion into Abyei box and protection of civilians under imminent threat. Lots of checkpoints were illegally erected along the highway linking Abyei with Mayen-Abun, commercial vehicles were overtaxed and road users continuously harassed. In this respect, the role of Gen. Akuei Ajuo, then commander of Division Three was too negative. He stationed some forces in areas of Athony and Ayuok under the command of then Col. Kuel Garang to do taxes on his behalf. The nature of those forces was so convoluted, some were Abyei Independent Brigade's ratters who hail from Twic, desperados and SSPDF's renegades from Division Three (3). Despite the undeniable activities of Twic's youth and their collaborators in those areas, Akuei forces were the most dangerous chancers who found Twic-Ngok conflict an auspicious environment to enrich themselves.

In what was believed to have been an escalation move, insurgents sneaked into Abyei Town on 29 September 2023, more than ten civilians were killed and another fourteen wounded at Nyinkuac market (Alsuk-Alshaabi), only two kilometres away from Indian Battalion base (INDBATT) at Rum-Ajak Deng Kuei, unfortunately, UNISFA did not come to the rescue. Furthermore, Twic armed youth attacked Alal County's areas of Kadhian and Malual Aleu on 13 November 2023, but Tiit-Bai repulsed the perpetrators and pursued them up to the border. On their way back, unidentified elements ambushed them and ran to the army barracks in Ayuok. This resulted in the burning of Ayuok base and killing of some SSPDF's personnel. As a response to this incident,

Gen. Akuei was said to have sent forces from Wunyiik in Awiel to avenge the killing of his unwarranted personnel in Ayuok.

As result, Abyei Civil Society Organization released a statement on 20 November 2023 as quoted below;

> *"The 19 November 2023 attacks resulted in killing of more than thirty-nine, including women and children, and injuring of thirty others. These massive attacks were from three directions (Angot of Rumamer County, Kadhian of Alal County and Wunpeeth village of Mijak County). The attacks were confirmed to have been carried out by some elements from Division Three of South Sudan Defense Forces (SSPDF). Reliable sources confirmed it that Maj. Gen. Akuei Ajuo Akuei of Division Three, dispatched two well-equipped platoons from Wunyiik in Awiel East to Abyei Area."* [63]

The Involvement of SSPDF in the intercommunal clashes between Ngok and Twic forced the head of UNMISS Nicholas Haysom to speak out urging South Sudan's Government to probe the killing of civilians in Abyei.

> *"The United Nations Mission in South Sudan called on the government to investigate the killing of seventy-five civilians in the disputed area of Abyei and the alleged*

---

63   United Nations Nicholas Haysom statement urging the Government of South Sudan to probe the killing in Abyei Area

involvement of South Sudan's People's Defense Forces (SSPDF) elements in the attacks. He added that: Most recently we have been concerned by reports of violence in Abyei Administrative Area and Warrap State which has claimed approximately seventy-five lives. I call upon the government to investigate these attacks and killings and to do what is necessary to reduce the tension between affected communities."[64]

Another escalation was in the form of assassinations of public figures. Twic armed militias backed by suspected elements from SSPDF ambushed a vehicle on Abathook -Agok road in Wunpeeth village on 19 November 2023. In the vehicle were some civilians and Hon. Mayot Kunit Miyen, former Minister of Physical Infrastructure, Public Utilities and Planning of Abyei Administrative Area. Hon. Mayot and the passengers on board were assassinated. On the same day, deadly attacks occurred in different villages, Ayuok, Athony, Malual-Aleu, Khàdhian, Nyiel, Angot, Wuncuei and Wunpeeth which resulted in the killing of forty-seven civilians and thirty-four wounded.

Another horrific assassination occurred in same Wunpeeth. an incumbent Deputy Chief Administrator, Hon. Noon Deng Nyok was ambushed and killed with all his crew on his way back to Abyei from Agok on 31 December 2023 at 5:00 PM. On the same route between Wunpeeth and Waucien, Agok Town Medical

---

64   Abyei Civil Societies Organization Statement on 7 January 2024

Assistant John Gier Jok was killed on 9 October 2024 around 3:00 PM. Gier was returning to his duty station in Agok after attending a workshop in Abyei Town. He was an example of a resilient and determined civil servant who insisted on doing his duty despite the risk. Gier was targeted to scare the residents in Agok and the surrounding areas, his stay in Agok was envisaged as a sort of resistance.

When fighting erupted between the communities of Apuk in Warrap State and Marialbai (Waau) of Western Bahar el Ghazal, President Kiir, unlike the case of Abyei and Twic in which his disinclination was apparent, directly intervened and called the governors of Western Bahar el Ghazal State, Warrap, Unity and Chief Administrators of Abyei and Ruweng. The meeting continued for two days from 10 to 11 January 2024, and resolved in the following:

1. The Governors of Warrap and Western Bahar el Ghazal States and the Chief Administrator of Abyei Special Administrative Area are directed to continue engaging politicians, military leaders, traditional leaders and other stakeholders in their respective areas to find a lasting peace between the two sisterly communities through initiation of dialogues to reconcile the two communities;

2. The relevant Security Institutions of the Country must deploy neutral forces to the conflict affected areas with clear operational orders to restore law and order;

3. The Security Forces must ensure that Mr. Gai Machiek, the Nuer Spiritual Leader is expelled from Ajak Kuac area in Warrap State and peacefully returned to either Unity State

or moved to another State of his choice within the Bahar el Ghazal Region, other than Warrap State and Abyei Special Administrative Area;

4. The Security Forces must also ensure that the Nuer youth present in Twic and Ngok areas are moved either back to the Nuer land or away from the areas of of conflict to States such as Northern Bahar el Ghazal, Western Bahar el Ghazal or Lakes;

5. The relevant Security Forces, Law enforcement agencies and Legal Institutions must ensure that any politician, person or group of politicians or persons who incites or incite violence on both or either sides of the respective communities, should be summoned and questioned or apprehended by the relevant authorities and where appropriate, arraign them in courts of law for Justice and tranquility to prevail. Land, borders and boundaries in the conflict affected areas of Twic, the Ngok Dinka, Apuk, Marialbai, including the question of Abyei box, must be put on hold and the leadership shall devise a peaceful means of resolving it accordingly. This order shall equally apply to other land, border and boundary related conflicts in other parts of the country;

6. The Governors of Warrap State, Western Bahar el Ghazal State and the Chief of Abyei Special Administrative Area are directed to engage the youth in their respective States or Areas to disengage and desist from violence, embrace peaceful coexistence including engaging them in agriculture, peace and development projects as well as income generating activities;

7. All the relevant Security Organs must continue to carry on arms search and peaceful disarmament of the civil population

in Warrap, Western Bahar el Ghazal States as well as other parts of the country;

8. All relevant Institutions should engage UNISFA to stick to its legal mandate.[65]

Twic's politicians were averse to those orders, particularly expulsion of Gai Machiek from their County. Losing Gai's services for Twic equated defeat. They, therefore, prodded the commonalities to demonstrate against President Kiir's orders. Furthermore, South Sudan People's Movement/Army (SSPM/A) Cdr. Gen. Stephen Buay Rolnyang issued a statement on 2 February 2024, claiming that Gai Machiek had nothing to do with the Twic-Ngok conflict and he called it victimisation ensnared by former National Congress Party's elements in Unity State:

> *"The Republican decree that President Kiir issued was not meant to resolve the conflict between Twic and Abyei. It's a clear indication that the President has acted in frustration based on the amount of pressure exerted on him by Tut Gatluak and the Governor of Unity State to return Gai Machiek to unity or be expelled from Warrap to another State of his choice as came in the decree of the president. The Conflict between Twic and Abyei can be resolved without Gai Machiek being a victim because he is not the one who caused the conflict between Twic and*

---

65   President Kiir's orders on the resolution of the conflict between communities of Twic, Ngok, Apuk and Marialbai

Abyei Communities. The president's decree issued on the pretext of resolving the conflict between Twic and Abyei is only meant to punish and return Gai Machiek to the Unity State and not to resolve the Twic-Abyei conflict."[66]

As I previously mentioned, understanding the nature of Twic-Ngok discordance requires one to have a clear picture of Unity State's internal sociopolitical dynamics. SSPM/A's position could be looked at from two intertwined contexts; the blood relation between the Commander of SSPM/A, Gen. Stephen Buay with Gai Machiek; and the rivalry between him and Joseph Monytueil, in addition to the implications of Tut Gatluak's revenge sentiment after his brother's assassination. On the other hand, people of Abyei envisaged both Gen. Stephen Buay and Gai Machiek from the perspective of their blood lineage with Twic.

Since late September 2023, Twic adopted a new strategy of taking violence to Abyei Town. They took advantage of Nuer Community's presence in Abyei and the featural similarities between Bul-Nuer and the Twic section of Duor whose members fluently speak Naath and have the same head marking style. This made it difficult for most of Ngok to differentiate who was from which, hence, insurgents infiltrated into Abyei Town. Twic, together with its collaborators, in a distinct violation of the president's orders, used their smuggled elements in Abyei Town. Shooting started at

---

66   SSPM/A Statement on response to President Kiir orders which requested Gai Machiek be returned to Unity State or any State of his choice in Bahar el Ghazal

Nyinkuac suburb on 27 January 2024, where Aneet IDPs from both Nuer and Ngok communities were residing.[67]

This unexpected mishap forced Nyinkuac's residents, particularly those in Maduol to flee to a UNISFA's site at Rum-Ajak seeking protection. Violence extended to the nearest thorps of Long-Athony and Nyinkuac market. However, Tiit-Bai managed to outset the attackers from Abyei Town, though it claimed dear lives of many strenuous youths. Some elements of Twic and Gai Machiek's insurgents attacked areas of Kadhian, Majbuong, Juljok and ambushed a vehicle carrying Ngok's IDPs from Abiemnthom to Rumamer County in Kol-ngol-nyang. Abyei Area as a whole was in great mayhem, the death toll reached more than fifty-two and sixty-four wounded; some with serious wounds died later in the hospital. But despite the sorrow wreaked on the people of Abyei and the surprising displacement of Bul Nuer innocent civilians, both communities exhibited much self-restraint, because they knew that incident was provoked by outsiders.

People were expecting more from governments of Abyei Special Administrative Area and Unity State to quieten the situation. Unfortunately, their administrative approach was unseemly astonishing. In the aftermath of Nyinkuac incidents, politicians from Bul Nuer and Ngok met in Juba to think of ways for positive intervention, and decided to form a Joint mechanism to visit the people on the ground. This move was welcomed by many political observers, because it served the mutual interest of the

---

67   Abyei's Civil Society Organisation & UNISFA's report on Nyinkuac incidents/27 January 2024

two communes. Deplorably, Chief Administrator of Abyei Area, Chol Deng Alak upset the applecart by declining to cooperate with the committee. Again, the composite nature of the local politics between Twic, Bul, Ngok and the central government negative intervention interrupted that perspicacious initiative.

The mission of the joint committee was hindered in a way believed to have been a political will of a transcendental authority. Others blamed VP Hussein's huge influence on Abyei Area's Chief Administrator, Chol Deng Alak. The way Bul Nuer residents were outcast from Abyei back to Mayom sent a negative signal as if there was a serious discord between the two communities. However, many political observers from Abyei believed that both Chol Deng Alak and Joseph Monytueil might have been forced to implement the order No. (4) of the resolution of the conflict between Twic-Ngok, Apuk and Marialbai communities. As apothegm indicates; *To understand the root cause of any problem, focus on who is profiting from the problem, not who is suffering from it*, both Ngok Dinka and Bul Nuer got disadvantaged from that intricacy underpinned by Juba-based politicians.

Ordinary Nuer youth who had been residing in Abyei since 2013, and the subsequent groups forced out of their lands by floods knew the whole thing was a setup by outsiders. Therefore, many left the area to avoid adding more complications to the already devastating scene. The Nyinkuac incident shocked Ngok community, it took some weeks for people to recover. In fact, the situation ran amok and confusion was the master of the scene, paralysing Tiit-Bai's deterrence system.

As a result, Gai Machiek insurgents' morale boosted and became active hither and thither without proper responses from Tiit-Bai. It was also reported that Gai Machiek's insurgents looted a warehouse belonging to one of the humanitarian organisations in Rumamer village on 2 February 2024. Some groups launched separate attacks on the 3rd and 4th of February respectively in Awolnhom, Minyang-Anyiel and Kadhian hamlets of Alal County, Tetak and Abathok villages of Mijak County. These heinous acts resulted in the killing of twenty people and raiding of seven hundred head of cattle and displacement of hundreds of people from their homes. All these unfortunate events took place within and around the jurisdiction of UNISFA's Ghanaian Battalion (GANBATT) in Awolnhom. Gai Machiek's insurgents again were said to have killed three civilians in Rumamer village and another one person in the bushes of Koladet in the eastern part of Abyei Town on 14 February 2024.

Attackers started another contemptible attitude of kidnapping people for the sake of ransom. This egregious terrorist behaviour began with the boy Deng Kuol Dupeir in April 2022, but developed into a phenomenon in January 2024, after elements of Twic section of Duor and Gai Machiek's insurgents secretly infiltrated to Abyei Town as ordinary Nuer residents. These morally decayed insurgents kidnapped four women on the road between Rumamer and Marial Achaak, on 10 January 2024, and they were finally released on ransom after being horrifically vexed and ravaged by hijackers. This savage act was replicated on 20th around Amiet market when ten women including a 10-year-old girl were reportedly abducted, no more details on this particular incident. As well, Mr. Diany Deng Agok, together with his two daughters were abducted at his garden in Amenth-bek just a few kilometres east of Abyei Town on 2 February 2024. They were held hostage for some days until Dr. Riek Machar Teny personally intervened and negotiated their release directly with Gai Machiek. Thanks to the First Vice President, Dr. Riek Machar, he did great work, despite the saddened traffic accident which shockingly took the life of Diany's elder daughter, Ayak! On the way to Rumamer which was designated as the point of delivery, captors heard sounds of vehicles then ordered the hostages to hide in the bush. It was a UNISFA patrolling convoy, then Ayak courageously decided to rescue the situation. She ran to the road waving to them, and unfortunately, one of UNISFA's vehicles knocked her down dead.[68]

---

68   Abduction of Dyany Deng Agok with his two daughters in their garden in Amenth-bek on 2 February 2024/Abyei Civil Society Organisation

Hon. Noon Deng Nyok, Deputy Chief Administrator of Abyei Special Administrative Area tragically assassinated on 31 December 2023 in Wunpeeth

Hon. Mayot Kunit Miyen, former Commissioner of Rumamer County and Minster of Physical Infrastructure and Public Utilities, tragically assassinated on 19 November, 2023 in Wunpeeth

CHAPTER 16

WAS THE CONFLICT PREVENTABLE?

"The current political and security status in Abyei was caused by entwined, multidimensional intricacy."

Bona Malwal's Anomalous Position on Abyei

Bona Malwal Madut, a veteran politician in the quondam Sudan and a notable public figure in Southern Sudan had been incessantly advocating for Abyei to be relinquished to Sudan. By doing this, Malwal was undermining many political factors related to Abyei's history which led to this current status. I do not want to re-narrate the genesis of the Abyei political question. However, many young politicians in South Sudan are baffled by Bona's anomalous stand on Abyei. Nowhere on earth does a compos mentis citizen reject a region where its people decided to join his or her country! It happens only in one situation, perfidy, where a certain individual decides to collaborate with a pugnacious country against his or her own for individualistic purposes.

Bona Malwal Madut's antagonistic position on Abyei was noxious, with no rational explanation that could justify his preposterous traitor-like stand.

I just want to give one example of a territorial dispute over a region in the Sudanese hodiernal politics—the case of Sudan's eastern town of Halaib. Irrespective of the different political and legal backgrounds between it and Abyei hoi polloi, academia, political parties and all Sudanese successive governments had one nationalistic view about Halaib. Even under whatever influence, you cannot find a politician who could say Halaib is an Egyptian territory and still be dealt with as a patriot. A nationalist can advise the competent authorities in a way that may not undermine his or her country's position, but reaching a level of advocating on behalf of a belligerent country like Sudan is a direct act of deliberate betrayal.

There is nothing static in human life, whether cultural concepts, social norms or even political status, everything is kinetic. Abyei peoples like other social groups in Southern Sudan had a history they feel proud of regardless of its vicissitudes. Bona Malwal Madut accepted all the political developments which occurred in Sudan from closed district ordinance when northern and southern Sudan were separately administered by condominium rule, reunited after the Juba conference in 1947 and again disunited after the comprehensive peace agreement in 2011, but wanted Abyei to remain statically in the 1905 status in Kordofan! The Comprehensive

Peace Agreement defines Abyei as the area of Ngok Dinka Nine Chieftaincies transferred to Kordofan in 1905, and that it shall be part of Kordofan in the north and Bahar el Ghazal in the south, managed directly under the presidency of the Republic of Sudan. It was this same agreement which gave Southern Sudan the right to self-determination, shifted Abyei from solely being considered a northern Sudan territory to a shared area between the north and south. The same CPA gave Abyei's people the right to determine the fate of their area, so I don't know why Bona Malwal Madut and his amateurish mentorees in Twic County of Warrap State insist on hostaging Abyei in the pre-CPA's era.

In his injudiciously written book, *Abyei of the Ngok Dinka: not yet South Sudan*, Bona Malwal has directly instigated the north and cautioned the south, by saying;

> *"The political elites of South Sudan had to be careful in their handling of the Abyei situation, not indicating that they wanted it to be an independent State, but also having a hidden ambition to separate geographical parts of Northern Sudan because of their strong cultural and blood affinity with the South."* [69] *(Bona 2017/ page 54)*

These last two lines above arguably put Bona Malwal in no category other than quislingsim—he was incontestably doing that with sanction from South Sudan's leadership of the day, otherwise, those political anarchists could have not been given such *laissez-aller.*

---

69   *Abyei of the Ngok Dinka: not yet South Sudan/*Bona 2017

Imagine, Bona Malwal Madut in this context envisages Abyei peoples as those who wanted to take a northern geographical territory to South Sudan! Bona focused on alienating Abyei, but unnoticeably gained himself the indisputable title of a turncoat. South Sudan cannot and will not be disadvantaged from Abyei joining it, but Bona thinks it will! He further mentioned

> *"In 2013 they conducted a fake referendum in Abyei without the support of Juba or Khartoum, although clearly Juba provided funding and logistics. They now think that the international community should recognise the result of that illegitimate referendum and should annex Abyei to South Sudan by force. The government in Juba is at least guilty of supporting a one-sided administration of Abyei by continuing to fund it without the support of Khartoum. This illegitimate administration wants Juba to occupy Abyei by force."* [70]

The objective of this roguish and skewed argument was to advocate on behalf of Sudan's government and warn the government of South Sudan to desist from pursuing the political cause of Abyei. Bona was oxymoronically driven by two conflicting factors; working on the pact between him and his bosom friends in Khartoum; and the fact at the innermost of his heart that Abyei is a Southern Sudan and Ngok territory.

Though he clearly confessed that Misseriya have never been

---

70   Ibid

permanent residents of Abyei, Bona still wanted Abyei to be Sudan's territory, not South Sudan. He says;

> *"On their part, the Misseriya Baggara Arabs have overreached themselves by claiming that Abyei is a territory that belongs to them. This is clearly false. I grew up in this area and when I was a child it was always unlikely that one would see a Baggara Arab in this area before December of any year. It was only during the dry season that we saw them on their horses, donkeys and oxen."* [71]

Twic Politicians' Acquisitive Propensity

The recent bellicose development in Abyei area was a wrongly-calculated attempt to achieve a mutual objective for the rapacious elites in the two Sudans. In cahoots with Khartoum, leadership in Juba, motivated by narrow political interests, had the eerie idea of dividing Abyei, northern part for Sudan and southern part for South Sudan. The political behaviour of the leadership in Sudan and South Sudan alluded to this, specifically during the reign of President Omar al Bashir. Furthermore, the wider space enjoyed by the protagonists of this ploy in South Sudan indicates that this had been backed by the inner circles. The theoretical basis for all claims recently devised by Twic County's officials were Bona Malwal's writings. Twic members of National Legislature are purportedly not naive to that degree, but knew that these

---

71   *Abyei of the Ngok Dinka: not yet South Sudan*/Bona 2017

mendacious, inflammatory demands represent the will of South Sudan's leadership of the day.

I was confused how national constitutional post holders could be naive to the extent of asking Abyei's Chief Administrator to redeploy UN's forces until I read it in their holy book; *Abyei of the Ngok Dinka: not yet South Sudan.* When Bona said:

> *"Abyei is currently an occupied territory, along with the territory of the Twic Mayardit Dinka community south of Abyei, occupiers being an Ethiopian contingent of the United Nations Peacekeeping Force. But there is no peace. The Ethiopians have become a UN occupation force. This foreign force imposed by Deng Alor Kuol when he was South Sudan's Minister for Foreign Affairs, has made life intolerable for the local population."*[72]

Bona Malwal did instigate Twic County's officials against UNISFA and was also believed to have been behind the brusque withdrawal of Ethiopian troops from Abyei shortly after conflict eruption between Twic and Ngok. Ethiopia did not tolerate that gross violation in Abyei box, they moved their armored equipment to Aneet market after it was partly burned. Shortly before the outbreak of conflict between Twic and Ngok, Sudan's government called for withdrawal of Ethiopian troops from Abyei following a political row implicated by renaissance damp and the border area of Fashaga, but that call was officially rejected by the Government

---

72   Ibid

of South Sudan. However, and after the eruption of the conflict between Ngok and Twic, President Kiir went to Addis Ababa and requested from the Prime Minister of Ethiopia, Dr. Abey Ahmed to withdraw his troops from Abyei. No justification was made for that wavering move up to this time of writing!

Bona Malwal has underhandedly inserted his toxic ideas by saying; Abyei is currently an occupied territory along with the territory of Twic Mayardit community.

He has indirectly goaded Twic community to claim Abyei's southern areas, hence, enthusiasts such as Charles Majak Aleer, Majok Yak Majok and Deng Tong Goch picked it up from there. Advancers of Twic-Ngok intrigue were members of sovereign institutions, and if not assured protection, they could not have dared to document such crimelike letters which preach violence. Since Governor Kon Manyiel's letter to President Kiir in 2018, and the nauseous subsequent letters written by Twic members of National Legislature and Twic County's Commissioner, National Government took no action. Therefore, inertia was considered a gesture of concession as came in the Sudanese paroemia;

'Silence is a sign of acceptance.'

The whole issue started when the family of Teeng Akuei of Kuac Anganya subsection of Amol claimed ownership of a thin piece of land adjacent to Mading-Jokthiang southwest of Agok Town. But after they discovered that this hoax was perfervidly supported by well-known reprobates, claims were inflated to include Agok Town where Aneet market is located. The stratagem never stopped there, but sections less averse to Ngok were beguiled to join, Twic sections of Adiang Mayom and Akoc-Thon were more friendly to Ngok. With them now in the game, claims inflated to include all Ngok areas south of the River Kiir. It could not have reached that destructive level, if contained in that stage, but as mentioned earlier, this conflict was driven by political and economic cupidity. Twic politicians wanted to incur into Abyei's agricultural lands of Rumamer and Alal Counties. Because President Kiir was put under Malwal Madut's armpit, Twic members of National Legislature continued in breaching the norms with impunity. Heteroclites rejected a region whose people decided to join South Sudan and subtly conspired to divide it with a pugnacious country! This errant situation should be made a case study, where leaders of a sovereign country reject a region whose people elected to join them, and again goaded one of the communities to grab parts from the region which they rejected! However, the *laissez-aller* enjoyed by Twic political abettors stood evident that this plot was underhandedly graced by Kiir's Administration. Dr. Carol was right in each word she said;

> *"Key individuals within the Jieng Council of Elders, and President Kiir himself, have strong ties to Khartoum. Their apparent surrender of control over Abyei is consistent with the favouring of Dinka from Greater Bahar el Ghazal, particularly the Twic, who have been lobbying to take part of the Abyei territory."* [73]

---

73   *Ethnocide as a tool for State Building*, Dr. Carol Berger

Conspiracy was so big, the northern part of Abyei has been ceded to Sudan which was strategically aiming for settling the Misseriya in it, while Twic community, beguiled by Bona Malwal Madut attacked the southern part of Abyei, what a freakish impetus!

Kiir Administration's Oscillating Policy on Abyei

The presumptuous politicians who initiated the conflict between the sisterly societies of Ngok and Twic have stated their unsubstantiated demands in an authoritative manner, hence, no official in the coterie of the current idiocrasy could claim to have not known. By this very fact, Twic politicians' move should have been reprimanded, yet all chose taciturnity! Abyei Protocol was negotiated by the same SPLM, the ruling party in South Sudan since independence in 2011 up to date. During the interim period when parties to the Comprehensive Peace Agreement disagreed on Abyei boundaries and sought international ruling in The Hague, it was SPLM that represented the people of Abyei. The then Deputy President for the autonomous government of Southern Sudan, Dr. Riek Machar Teny led the SPLM delegation to The Hague, where Abyei boundary (Box) was determined and the ruling was recognised by the Government of Sudan and Government of Southern Sudan.

Abyei Protocol states clearly that southern boundaries as they stood on 1 January 1956, shall remain inviolate until the realisation of the final status. Again, the referendum of Southern Sudan was based on the same border line of 1 January 1956. I was the translator for Carter Center's team of northern Warrap (Twic), and Abyei. When Abyei referendum was postponed, Carter Center continued to observe the postponement's related implications. But in Twic our team roamed the polling centres all over Twic County except Pan-Nyok Payam, due to inaccessibility. There were no polling centres in places now claimed by Twic members of National Legislature, Agok, Akur, Marol-Diil, Miyen Jech, Athony, Malual-Aleu and Kadhian. The reason was that these areas are all in Abyei Box, even Bona Malwal's constituency, Ajak-Kuac adjacent to Abyei from the South had no polling centre. The nearest centres to Ajak-Kuac from east and south were Agok-Nyang and Mapeir respectively if areas in Abyei Box now claimed by some Twic politicians were their territories, what prevented a referendum from being conducted in them?

There is a claim that there was an agreement between Bashir and Kiir regarding Abyei issue, which may surface in the future. However, the same tactics which were used by Khartoum's successive governments are now being applied by the government of South Sudan. Kiir's Administration usage of a juxtaposed community as a tool while underpinning intricacies from behind, SSPDF's involvement in the conflict, and the surrender of Twic county to militias affiliated with them were all spiteful interventions!

Two ASAA'S senior officials were assassinated in dubious circumstances, a former Minister for Physical Infrastructure and an incumbent Deputy Chief Administrator. Unfortunately, National Government ignored those odious incidents, it neither formed an investigation committee, nor issued a condemnation statement or even a message of condolence.

President Kiir's real face and the vehement sentiment he had been harbouring against the Ngok people of Abyei was revealed during this conflict.

However, boundaries between Abyei and Warrap shall continue to be considered international, unless a resolution on final status of Abyei Area is reached. There is nothing changed. It was the same provincial borderline between former provinces of Kordofan and Bahar el Ghazal. Yes, there are disputes in some parts of the borders between Sudan and South Sudan, but no registered case of disputation on Abyei southern border between Kordofan and Bahar el Ghazal. If such a case existed, it could have arisen during negotiations on the resolution of Abyei conflict in Naivasha, or during Arbitration in The Hague.

Regarding the question of whether the conflict between Ngok and Twic was preventable, the answer is yes. Twic-Ngok conflict was, and is not insoluble, but could provocateurs solve a problem of their own making? Kiir's led government took anesthetic administrative procedures with no genuine intention to cease the conflict. However, both Ngok and Twic patriots and patriotesses must work effortfully to restore serenity to their communities.

PART 6

REVIVIFICATION OF NGOK-TWIC RELATIONS

Despite the severity of the catastrophe, I believe that Twic-Ngok relations could be refixed, because the fight was not theirs

CHAPTER 17

NGOK AND KUAC
THROUGHOUT HISTORY

Kuac and Ngok had been living peacefully for nearly a century now since it was annexed to Akuar. No registered vendettas between them except one minor event popularly known as Tong Michar/ Michar battle which occurred in the mid-1950s. This battle was between the age sets of Acuil and Wuor of Diil and their peers in Kuac subsection of Ayuang, not even the whole Kuac and Diil Chieftaincy. The case of today's Twic section of Kuac which is now called after Madut Ring, the father of the renowned politician Bona Malwal Madut, is a bit unique. This subsection of Jieng was, until recent history, part of Ngok Dinka of Abyei. Though it has been almost a century since Kuac was administratively detached from Ngok, more similarities between them are still recognisable. The last generations of Kuac which were head-marked had the same facial features and the dialect never changed much, although a slight twist of the tongue is observable due to demographic exposure. No written script precisely indicates the time and reasons of detaching Kuac from Ngok and annexing it to Akuar subsection of Twic. However, oral history and a few contemporary writings, particularly Bona Malwal Madut Ring's writings, can help in excavating the history of Kuac and its relationship with Ngok people of Abyei.

According to Ngok narrative, it is a question of unanimity that Kuac section was part of Ngok until the mid-1930s under the administration of Kon Tingloth, the grandfather of Diil's current Chief Arop Kuol Kon Tingloth.[74] Opinions diversify only in what the reasons and motives were for the annexation of six subsections of Kuac to Akuar in Twic. However, it is generally believed to have not been ordered by a government authority or done using coercive measures. These factors could be classified into two; social and administrative. Akuar was minority in terms of the population compared to other sections of Twic such as Amol Bol Chol Nyuol and Adiang Cier Rihan. It is said that Akuar did not qualify to have a separate administration of its own during the establishment of Southern Sudan native administrations in 1930s, hence Juuk Chom requested from Kuol Arop to give him his people whose area is adjacent to Akuar (Kuac) in order to qualify for a separate chieftaincy. When Ngok Court was officiated separately by colonial administration in the mid-1930s in Kordofan, Kuol Arop accepted the request of his friend Juuk Chom and allowed his

---

74   Arop Kuol Kon Tingloth, the Chief of Diil Chieftaincy

people of Kuac to be administered under Akuar's administration in the South. It is believed that Kuol Arop was also facing challenges in effectively managing Kuac section due to geographical factors, particularly during rainy seasons. Thanks to the swampy terrain, Kuac people were said to have been evading paying taxes in their remote areas which were the southernmost territories of Ngok Dinka of Abyei.

Another reason known to Kuac and Ngok was social; Kuol Arop had friendly relations with the family of Juuk Chom. Alueldit Juuk, the mother of Yai Kuol Arop and the sister of Lang Juuk had linked the two families. It is no secret in Twic that Kuac five sections which are today called after Madut Ring and the other subsection of Anganya that branched away from them and joined Twic subsection of Amol Bol Chol Nyuol were natively Ngok Dinka of Abyei. *(Deng Teng, the father of Kuac Anganya's current chief was said to have been initiated in Anyar Diil Age Group)*

What should be emphasised here, regardless of whatsoever reasons that might have motivated Kuol Arop to give his people of Kuac to Akuar, is that it was done in good faith according to general understanding of the day. But if looked at from the perspective of today's modern politics, there was no difference between detachment of Kuac from Ngok and transfer of Abyei area to Kordofan. Both decisions were arbitrarily taken with no prior consultation with the people. The first was done by native administration (Kuol Arop) and the latter by colonial administration (Condominium rule).

It is worth mentioning that when Abyei was transferred to northern Sudan province of Kordofan in 1905, Kuac was part of

Ngok Dinka community. Ngok and Kuac shared history and it is very unfortunate that intellectuals of these two sisterly communities do not intend to surface that exact epoch when Kuac was unlinked from Ngok which hugely contributed to shaping their politics today. The influence of this history is apparent in Bona Malwal Madut's character. Thus, he became a bigot arbiter in the Abyei political question. Bona's characteristics were arguably side-effects of those circumstances.[75]

Chiefly, I'm thankful to Bona Malwal Madut for shedding some light on the dim pages of this important history, regardless of his motives and the intentional distortions he made in it. In the Preface of his book; *Abyei of the Ngok Dinka: not yet South Sudan* he mentioned;

> *"My own life and that of my family have been close to the Ngok Dinka people. At one time, before the traditional leadership of the Ngok Dinka people decided to lead their community to Kordofan in Northern Sudan, my own section, known as Kuac Madut Ring— after my father, Madut Ring, who became the first chief of Kuac-Angnya—refused to join the Ngok to become part of Northern Sudan. My father and Chief Deng Majok Kuol Arop of the Ngok Dinka people of Abyei were contemporaries, being initiated (head-marked) on the same day to be recognised as Dinka adults. The departure of the Ngok people to Kordofan left the Kuac people*

---

75   Abyei between two Sudans

of Twic in South Sudan without a chiefdom of their own, something my father struggled for. Finally, it was granted, but by this time the national politics of Sudan had become unstable, with South Sudan and Northern Sudan enmeshed in a war of independence." [76]

As mentioned earlier, Bona's psychological setting was extremely shaped by events to do with relations between today's section of Kuac which became part of Twic and his quondam community, the Ngok Dinka of Abyei. What he asserted in the above quotation are facts, but skewed to comply with his assertions. Saying his life and that of his family have been closed to Ngok is a soft acknowledgement that they were part of Ngok. Then he twisted it by claiming that his section *refused to join the Ngok to become part of Northern Sudan.*[77] When Abyei Area was transferred to Kordofan by colonial rulers, people had not been consulted on whether they liked the decision or not. Moreover, transfer happened during the time of Arop Biong, the grandfather of Deng Majok who was not coetaneous with Madut Ring, the father of Bona Malwal. Bona also said that his father became the first chief of Kuac Anganya after they were attached to Akuar, but did not mention who their Chiefs were before his father! There is a clear anachronism (mis-history) in the account of dates and characters in his narrative. Bona distorted the history to veil the fact that his section of Kuac was transferred

---

76   Bona Malwal 2017

77   Ibid

in 1905 to Kordofan as part of Ngok community and that their annexation to Twic was a local arrangement between Chief Kuol Arop and Juuk Chom of Akuar subsection of Twic community. The consultation he is alluding to was in 1952 which he (Bona) attended with his father and that was during the time of Deng Majok, and Kuac section was already detached from Ngok by then.

Bona Malwal had also admitted when he said that his father was initiated together with Deng Majok, because people of different tribes cannot be initiated in one age-set. Deng Majok age group is Turok-dit of Abior chieftaincy which had been head-marked approximately during the 1910s. The name Turok is derived from Turkey. In Ngok Dinka of Abyei, each Chiefdom has its age set, the rite of head-marking was done accordingly and each group knows its counterparts in the other chiefdoms. For instance, the age set of Turok in Abior Chieftaincy counterparts the age group of Acuil in Diil Chieftaincy, Chief Madut Ring was probably initiated in Acuil. Again, he unconsciously confessed his section of Kuac was part of Ngok Dinka of Abyei by saying; *The departure of the Ngok people to Kordofan has left Kuac people without a chiefdom of their own.*[78] It is presumably believed that Kuac was annexed to Akuar without conduct of a popular consultation exactly as happened to people of Abyei when their administration was transferred to Kordofan.

There in Twic, the new relocatees (Kuac) were socioculturally incongruous having different marks at their foreheads and speak different dialect. The challenges they faced were all about cultural

---

78   Bona Malwal 2017

dissimilarity, this incongruity was the reason that motivated the people of Kuac to demand a chiefdom of their own. For Chief Madut Ring who attended the 1952 conference in Abyei, the administrative reinstatement of Abyei's Court to Southern Sudan could have regained him and his people a sense of kinship, because they were oddly placed where they were feeling so peculiar. Despite the fact that he was given a position of Deputy Chief of Akuar Chieftaincy, Chief Madut Ring's feeling was exactly as Ngok's pro-south leaders who were forced to stay in Kordofan against their will, particularly after 1952. I am quite sure if he (Chief Madut Ring) was to be alive now, he could not have been repugnant as his son. Bona's feeling extremely flipped from sense of belonging to inveterate intent for vengeance. His trend is retributive, because what he mistakenly envisaged as an advantage, being in Kordofan, enjoyed by Abyei's leadership, turns obverse today. For Bona Malwal, annexing his people to Akuar was disadvantageous, but it is now a privilege as South Sudan became an independent country.

CHAPTER 18

YESTERN'S BROTHERS TURNED ENEMIES TODAY

"This is a trace of brethren's backsides, only I don't know what they were discussing."
- Dinka Proverb

Both communities of Kuac and Ngok have to rationally chew it over, because the machination is aiming at wrecking their historical brotherly relations to be replaced with scathing repulsion that would benefit none, only the ensnarers. Relations between Kuac and Ngok had incorrectly been reflected to their neighbours to the South, as if there was genuine animosity. This slit, through which entanglers got into Kuac-Ngok relations, was opened by Bona Malwal Madut. His diuturnal negative stand on Abyei's political cause is what is now being exploited. Irrespective of sociocultural ties between Kuac and Ngok, specifically Diil, there is no rationale for turning peaceful neighbourliness to adversity. Geographical locations are unaltered realities, they inevitably link the people whether they coexist peacefully or not. Kuac and Ngok were one community, hence should be bound by brotherly ties rather than conflicts.

It's contrary to universal logic to allow others to spoil one's own life. None in this political absurdity got severely devastated more than Kuac and Ngok. When fighting intensified, Diil and Kuac areas were turned battlefields and most border thorps bore the brunt of that unnecessary vandalism. The traditional boundaries between some subsections of Kuac and some clans of Diil such as Pabukjaak, Pajook, Paguiny and Payaadh are known and people are strongly connected through intermarriages.

Bona's position against the Ngok people of Abyei should be dealt with as an isolated phenomenon. It should not be claimed by Twic, Kuac or even his direct family of Chief Madut Ring, because his motive has no linkage with innocent communities of Twic and Ngok.

Kuac community should distance itself from this involution in which it has been used as a shield. It is apparent that this exaggerated territorial claim was engineered by politicians from Twic sections which administratively hosted Kuac. Amol hosted Kuac Anganya and the other five sections were under Akuar. It is injudicious to surrender oneself to be used as a tool for fulfilling another's avarice. When Twic State's Governor Atem Madut Yak erected illegal tax points at Athony on the highway which connects Abyei with Mayen Abun and Mabuony in Agok on the road linking Mijak Kol with Aneet market, Kuac community was not the direct beneficiary of those revenues.

The resources were for the whole state, it is so bogglesome as to why Kuac accepted to be used against her sisterly community, the Ngok Dinka of Abyei. Peaceful coexistence in Abyei was wisely invested by all the neighboring communities, Twic, Awiel, Abiemnom and Unity State. People were normally trading between Amiet, Aneet and their respective areas. It is wise for Kuac community to abandon this problematic political attire and tailor another one that would fit it as Kuac. Each community has its neighbours and must be heedful in keeping that neighbourhood peaceful.

It is therefore significant for Kuac to re-evaluate this unwise political business which was cunningly assigned to spearhead. As I mentioned above, locations are not transferable, as Agok is more exposed to Kuac, Turalie and Awieng are also safer than Tongliet, Yomboldit, Anyiel and Ajak Kuac. If people learn, relearn and unlearn from their experiences, Kuac and Ngok must have learned from the 2022 epoch. Some families in both communities remained only with female members, youth have killed themselves ruthlessly for no genuine reasons. It is unfortunate that such Boeotian politicians be allowed to ruin the life of innocent communities of Twic and Ngok.

If this was not a real political collusion, how could those goons who thought it up replicate what Sudan and Misseriya had been doing in the northern part of Abyei? The intriguers of this stratagem wanted to simulate the same political game which Sudan had used for decades, a proxy war steered by Riverine Political Elites from Omdurman and used Misseriya AJ'aaira as instruments.

Other sections of Misseriya which do not have borders with Ngok Dinka were invited in, but when the game breaks off, it is AJ'aaira who always bears the brunt. The same would apply for Kuac, most of the entanglers of this involution are not direct neighbours to Ngok, they enjoy beneficial proximity with their other neighbours. So why did Kuac and Ngok allow their brotherly relations to be fordone by others?

There is no territorial dispute between Ngok and Twic, the root causes of this conflict are socio-economic. Twic Area had, since time immemorial, been intermittently facing famine, this was not because its people were lazy, but their terrain is swampy and hard to cultivate using primitive tools.

Ngok's area had been the back yard and a rescuer for Twic in this respect, but there were other ways Ngok benefited from Twic too. During dry seasons when grasses become scarce, Ngok herders take their cattle to Twic. That was how our forefathers cooperated and cared for themselves to overcome the challenges wreaked upon them by nature. However, there are so many ways to deal with this perennial problem of hunger today more than in the past, it only requires security be maintained and responsible political elites to explore potential solutions for the problems which face their communities.

People from different subsections of the neighbouring communities were placidly employing the land using their primitive tools. In Alal County for instance, members of neighbouring communities of Adiang Mayom, Akoc-Thon, Awan and Awiel East have been peacefully coexisting, hence utilising the land smoothly. Moreover, eastern parts of Twic such as Kuac, Amol and Akuar were sharing with their brothers in Rumamer County. Not only them, but some individuals from Aguok and Apuk were also there. If modern agricultural methods were applied, Abyei Area could be a food basket to the whole region of Bahar el Ghazal and beyond, exactly like the northern Upper Nile's area of Renk. Instead of deducing ways to effectively utilise Abyei's pristine lands, reprobate politicians incited communities against one another! Killing others for one's own survival is a jungle indulgence, but enhancing people's capacities for collective survival is a human sagacity. Twic and Ngok communities should not have allowed themselves to be hoodwinked by corrupt politicians who incessantly wanted to pass on their old Sudan's prepackaged misconceptions and experiences.

Despite the fact that many were misled and turned war bellicists in the recent conflict, I am sure youth, particularly the educated ones, have realised how war was so burdensome. It is therefore significant for both communities to discourage it. Youth have to deduce peaceful mechanisms and deescalate violence as a mean of solving the problems. As prophets of doom had found reckless jingoes to execute their intrigues, peace lovers have to have some degree of exuberance in order to get their communities refixed. It may involve some challenges, because benefactors of bellicism would not tolerate that. But is it not worth it? It is honourable to expose one's life to risk in search for peace rather than losing it in meaningless battles.

Crisis Misreading & Mismanagement

Ngok and Twic, like any other neighbouring communities, have their beautifully unique ways of humorously befooling and bullying themselves and that is normal. For instance, Agar people of Rumbek and Atout of Yirol fabricate funny things against each other, same thing between Bari and Mundari, Bor and Aliap people of Aweirial, but I wonder when I stumbled upon this ill-used, and inflammatory term of *historical grievances* in Aneet's Facts Finding Committee Report! So, what could be those historical grievances? Findings (No 6 & 7) in AFFC report, read as follows;

> 6. *"The committee identified that the longstanding historical and social grievances between the two communities which were not addressed contributed to the deterioration of relations.*
> 7. *The Committee noted that the employment processes in ASAA were discriminatory towards non-Ngok as the applicants were required to identify themselves with one of the nine Ngok Chiefdoms."*

The committee did not elaborate enough on the alleged historical and social grievances which appeared in its report. A core sensitive finding as such should not have been opaquely inserted in such generality. Respondents must have further been probed in order to clearly state those alleged grievances. Twic and Ngok communities had never been under one administration, because geographically, they are separate entities except Kuac whose historical and social ties with Ngok I talked in detail about, but the other Twic sections of Akuar, Adiang, Amol and Akoc-Thon are just neighbours to Ngok. There is no recorded disputation in the history between Twic section of Adiang and Anyiel of Ngok or between Abior and Akoc-Thon. Adiang and Akoc-Thon are the bordering communities to Abyei from south and southwest divided by Alaal stream. The adjacent inhabited area at the southern bank of Alaal stream is called Makuac Alaal, which belongs to Twic. Makuac Alaal at the northern shore belongs to Anyiel chiefdom of Abyei Area. Neither Adiang nor Akoc-Thon had ever claimed any area north of Alaal stream, as with the other two sections of Amol and Akuar the recent claim on Abyei Southern Kiir areas was politically motivated.[79]

If what came in the AFFC report was about grievances that might have occurred after the Comprehensive Peace Agreement, it is Ngok that has grudges against the Twic community according to Chief Bagat Makuac Abiem's statement to Aneet's Facts Finding Committee. What AFFC termed as discrimination *in employment process* in Abyei Special Administrative Area was also doubtful and just a smear-campaign. It was not clear in which sector the alleged discrimination happened, because the system of governance in the Republic of South Sudan is decentralisation. Each state employs its residents according to South Sudan's laws. Unless a post was publicly advertised and no candidate from that respective state qualified for it, then any other South Sudanese who meets the requirements can be contracted as an individual contractee or through a secondment by his or her institution, be it state or national. South Sudanese are only stakeholders in the National Government, each state and administrative area has full rights to prioritise the employment of its residents. *(Residents here*

---

79   Akonon Ajuong Deng Tiel, Chief of Anyiel Chieftaincy

are those recognised by the local authorities of that particular State/
Administrative Area regardless of their ethnic or tribal backgrounds)

It could be a bit different in the private sector where companies
and organisations operating in South Sudan are mostly international with most of them headquartered in the capital and choose
any state or administrative area as operational site. Yet, if a position
is in Awiel or Warrap for instance, priority must be given to local
residents of that state. This is the reason why residence certificates
were requested from local applicants to prove they are residing in
Abyei Special Administrative Area, hence deserving of priority as
a local resident. No one was requested to abandon their ethnicity, section or subsection. I remember in 2018, a row arose in
Abyei regarding this matter, local residents complained that people
from Warrap generally and Twic in particular were dominating
the organisations, *Medicins Sans Frontieres* (MSF) in particular.

Local complaints about outsiders' dominance over NGO positions is not an isolated phenomenon for Abyei; similar cases arose
in different areas, for instance, Maban area in Upper Nile, Ruweng
Administrative Area and Awiel. Such problems are there in most
states in South Sudan.

There is also the general sentiment that Equatorians are dominating the NGOs, specifically, Acholi, Madi, Kuku and Moro,
however, it should not reach a level of physical violence. What
intensified the case between Ngok and Twic was that job seekers
who hail from Twic were hinting that Aneet is their home, hence
considered themselves not just normal residents, but natives.

All the reasons mentioned in the AFFC report were not
enough to cause such destructive conflict between neighbouring

communities! Twic community as a whole and Kuac in particular, have been badly exploited and used as a political shield by warmongers in Kiir's administration against Ngok people of Abyei. SSPDF bizarre interventions in the Twic-Ngok conflict apparently indicates that Kiir's government was behind the wheel. There was no reason for sending all those undefined forces to Agok without a clear mandate. The Tiger forces which were sent on 10 October 2022, have been there, but prevented no attacks and never moved an inch to pursue the culprits. Horrendous assassination of senior officials of Abyei Special Administrative Area happened in Wunpeeth just a few kilometres away from forces base in Agok Town.

Another force was unofficially deployed by Gen. Akuei Ajou at Ayuok and suspected to have been harbouring elements from Twic armed youth, while other forces in police uniform were brought from Juba and stationed in Mayen-Abun, a border Town between Ngok and Twic. These police forces were said to have been given a mandate for patrolling the commercial highway linking Abyei with Warrap. Furthermore, on 28 March 2024, SSPDF force commanded by Maj. Gen. Joseph Kwai Ajak was sent to Agok again without a specific mandate while the previous force of Tiger was not redeployed. This excessive deployment of unwarranted forces has, instead of restoring peace, become a source of insecurity in Agok and South Kiir areas as a whole.

In continuation of their devious plan, a serious assassination attempt transpired in Agok Town of Rumamer County when Hon. Minister of Local Government and Law enforcement, Abionweing Majith Diing was coming from Juba on 7 April 2024, and received by Rumamer County's Commissioner, Hon. Ayuel Kiir Chol. As she was seated in a guest house near Agok Airstrip, a group of SSPDF soldiers opened fire unexpectedly on the two officials which resulted into killing of three personnel from the protection team including one of the Chief Administrator's guards. Rumamer County's Commissioner was injured together with four other personnel. Forces showed loutish conduct which signified their ill-intentions. Ministers' luggage was looted and the Commissioner's premises where he used to conduct his duties as the top official of that administrative jurisdiction were occupied right away by SSPDF's force.

It was inscrutable why institutions of the same government treat each other in such a ruthless way! This incident proved beyond doubt that SSPDF's presence in Agok was in line with the wider machination of displacing Ngok from South Kiir Areas and Aneet in particular.

CHAPTER 19

WAS IT REALLY
BETWEEN TWIC & NGOK?

*To outlandish intruders who have been fanning the
conflict, stop it. You don't know how mixed is the blood
of Twic and Ngok*

The message here is unadornedly direct to my beloved communities of Twic and Ngok. I autonomously feel morally obliged to call for peace as I toughly criticised the warniks during the intense days of the conflict, particularly Twic Members of National Legislature and their gaffer, Bona Malwal Madut. As some eccentrics chose to be killers of their own people, straight-hearted fellows have to thwart their ill-deeds and rescue the communities from such reckless intent. This conflict started with Bona Malwal Madut's insidious political theorisation that Abyei is a Sudanese territory and that the Government of the Republic of South Sudan should not allow its relations with Sudan to be imperilled because of Abyei. Following the early surrender of Abyei file to Sudan, Bona's acolytes picked it up from there when they knew that Abyei could be an easy prey to engorge. Twic's MPs, prodded by Malwal Madut, wrote to President Kiir demanding him to relocate five Chiefdoms of Abyei from their native areas on the southern side of River Kiir to the northern part of Abyei. This move which served as a water-testing tactic, was not supported by Kiir's Administration. It could have been aborted at that stage, but President Kiir was standing neck-deep in that convolution, therefore never dissuaded Twic's Members of National Legislature to stop their precarious attempts.

Up to this level, Twic as a community was not structurally involved until it reached a perilous level of physical violence, then children of ordinary people were used as tools in the fight. Is this not kind of befooling and exploitation? In the whole long period, more than two years now, I never heard a son of any of the politicians who did intrigue the conflict to have fallen in the fight. Their kids are joyfully staying in East Africa and beyond enjoying quality education and good health services. After hundreds, if not thousands of youths from communities of Twic, Ngok and some Bul Nuer from both sides perished, Kiir's government deployed contingents of troops in Agok Town without a clear mandate. Young people were killed in vain and considered as just experimental elements in a political laboratory while politicians who fueled the conflict were pompously living their luxurious life in Juba with no regard! Irrespective of how this conflict will end, Ngok and Twic would remain the only losers, therefore, it's a direct ethical duty on children of Twic and Ngok's necks to constructively intervene and rid their communities of this political exploitation.

This conflict, apart from precious lives which were unnecessarily lost, material properties destroyed, and social fabric ruined, has worsened the state of pauperism and destitution in Ngok and Twic communities. Ordinary people were exchanging benefits in peaceful environments, thus managing to overcome the enormous challenges inflicted on them by economic hardship, but look now at what Boeotian political elites have done? In fact, our people on the ground were genuine and immaculate, all these ill-begotten ideas conjured into their minds were byproducts of war bellicists. The early reconciliatory attempts, initiated first in Awiel by Facts Finding Committee and the other two conferences facilitated by UNISFA, Concordis and some national organisations in Western Bahar el Ghazal's capital, were bedeviled by the same politicians. It is high time for progressive forces to ask the outlanders to get out their shanks and stop intruding themselves into Twic- Ngok internal affairs. If Twic and Ngok seek an ironclad peace to ameliorate the situation in their communities, it must be pursued away from political influences of Juba-based entanglers.

I am quite sure that young generations have required know-how to lead their societies out of these disproportionate conditions. For peace lovers who would accept the challenge, it requires no politicisation, but integrity and courage for telling the truth even if it controverts the wrongly defined interest of one's own commune. Because real intellectuals do not act in ostrich ways, but influence their societies by telling them the fact blatantly as it is, because an ill-interest is a no interest. The bona fide men and women who shall accept to lead this noble mission would probably face some challenges in correcting their people's minds, but nothing is above the truth as apothegm goes;

'Wrong is wrong even if everyone is doing it, and right is right even if no one is doing it.'

The deleterious policy adopted by Kiir's Administration on Abyei was not a unanimous position supported by all South Sudanese political forces. Abyei is and shall be nowhere other than South Sudan. Bona Malwal's anti-Ngok scheme which tends to trade away Abyei to Sudan would fade away when another leader takes over, whether from SPLM or any other South Sudanese patriotic political parties. In addition to that, influence of Omar Al-Bashir's former adjutants who emulated his policies and deviously incited Twic innocent community against their brothers in Abyei, shall end in a lamentable way if they fall from favour.

The economic-related challenges that people face in Abyei and some neighbouring areas such as northern Warrap, Gogrial and Awiel can be dealt with administratively. As I mentioned elsewhere in this book, Abyei's soil is fit for agriculture. If used properly, it could feed the whole region of Bahar el Ghazal, Western Upper Nile and beyond, besides oil and other natural resources. However, the full reinstatement of Abyei area to South Sudan should be made a priority and ardently campaigned for first by neighbouring states to Abyei; Northern Bahar el Ghazal, Warrap, Ruweng Administrative area and Unity State. Communities of these states should first stretch hands to Abyei and effectively engage in advocating for its return to South Sudan. You cannot expect far communities such as Madi and Acholi in the southernmost part of the country to sympathise with the people of Abyei while their direct neighbours and the region where it was detached from are muted!

I am all hope that Twic, Warrap and South Sudanese well-informed generations shall flip this scenario from predating the Ngok people of Abyei to advocating for their political cause.

Since the eruption of this conflict idiotically misnamed as a problem between Ngok and Twic, I never ever blamed the youth, because they were nurtured with wrong narratives. Therefore, I encourage the educated young men and women in Twic and Abyei to spontaneously get onstage and fast track awareness campaigns in their societies. It is undeniable that this conflict has caused deep wounds on Twic and Ngok social body, but there is no better way other than telling the truth and directing people's anger at the idiotic warmongers.

The optimum way for peaceniks to avenge, is not through violent revengeful reactions, but by disarming the warniks of their weapons which are misinformation and hatred. Plebs should be re-brainwashed and taught how advantageous is peaceful coexistence. Normally, ordinary people do not have capacity to accurately analyse the political state of affairs, therefore, driving commonality's attention back should be a responsibility of the living forces in the communities. The sadistic character of those politicians who needlessly invited a plague-like calamity to Ngok and Twic peaceful communities must publicly be demonised and condemned.

There is no social progeny whether in Twic, or Ngok which death did not enter into its household. This could have been avoided if not for the slinky agendas of those blunt politicians. The common interest for the two communities is peace, and anyone found flying against, must be outcast and considered a strange bird. Peace must come and I believe it will. Despite the severity of the catastrophe, it is possible, because this tussle was only imposed on Twic and Ngok by some abettors, the likes of Charles Majak Alier, Majok Yak Majok and the rest of their doctrinaire cahoots who dogmatically believe in Bona's inexpedient expansionary philosophy.

PART 7

THE UNFINISHED MISSION

The issue of Abyei was not only Sudan's political intransigence, but rather, Kiir Administration's vacillating policy on Abyei.

CHAPTER 20

THE FATE OF
A MIS-NEGOTIATED DEAL

Some influential circles in the west misconceived the root cause of the conflict between the North and South Sudan as solely a religious and sociocultural incongruity. They did not consider the economic aspects and the gap created by uneven developmental policies, but regarded it as dissonance between Islamic, Arabic North and a black, African mostly Christian South Sudan. However, the controversy between the North and South Sudan was a multifaceted matter which could be summarised into two; religious and ethnocultural degradation and rejectionism and contention over political powers and economic resources. To control the most resourceful areas, distortive political decisions were made, particularly during the militaristic regimes of Gen. Ibrahim Abboud (1958-64) and Gen. Jaafar Mohammed Nimieri

(1969-85). When a report reached President Abboud that copper was explored in Kafia Kenji in the most northern west of Southern Sudan's Province of Bahar el Ghazal, he manipulatively used his executive powers and annexed Kafia Kenji to a northern Sudan province of Darfur in 1960. New maps were drawn to officiate that spurious decision and it was renamed as Hoforat el Nihas, a translation for the hole of copper. This is only an example to betone the fact that resources were at the centre of the political crisis between Southern and Northern Sudan.

Conflict over Abyei embodied the core of quondam Sudan's political crisis; identity, political and economic exploitation were fundamental factors that caused deep-seated acrimony, polarising the Sudanese population across ethnicity, classism and regionalism. However, Ngok people's umbilical cord with their kith and kin in South Sudan is uncuttable, they had long ago exhibited unbridled desire to rejoin their kinfolks. It was manifestly clear that Khartoum's successive administrations favoured Misseriya, however, that partiality had exposed Ngok ethnocultural peculiarity in the north. Despite the fact that Riverine Elites had been using ethnic, religious and sociocultural affinities to delude Misseriya, their political spuriosity was unveiled recently when they described Misseriya, Rizigat and all the nomadic Arabs of Kordofan and Darfur as hoodlums and peregrines (wandering Arabs/ Arab al shataat) following the conflict between Gen. Mohammed Hamdan Dagglo of the Rapid Support Forces (RSF) and Gen. Abdal Fatah Al Burhan of Sudan's Armed Forces (SAF).

Since Abyei Area was transferred to Kordofan Province by the Condominium rule, Ngok people of Abyei were conscientious of their ethnocultural dissimilarity in that northern Province of Kordofan, therefore, insisted to administer their affairs (traditional Court) separately from Misseriya's courts. It is evident that the international community, particularly leading countries which brokered the CPA, did not get down to the nitty -gritty of the Sudanese politics. As described by Prof. Douglas Johnson that; *focusing on resolving the Southern problem only, the international mediators failed to recognise the common political, economic, and cultural issues of marginalisation that linked large parts of the border region to the wider war.* [80]

The case of Abyei and the other two regions of South Kordofan and South Blue Nile were not heeded to enough as Prof. Douglas H. Johnson adjudged them to have been just secondary matters whether for Sudan, international guarantors or even SPLM; *Abyei was largely an afterthought that inadequately addressed the main issues confronting the peoples of the area.*[81] The US's proposal which was presented to the parties by its special envoy Senator John Danforth aimed primarily at breaking the impasse. The United States was so obsessed with achieving the peace by all means. When Senator Danforth told the parties to; *Take it or leave it,* it was a message to the Government of Sudan and Sudan People's Liberation Movement that they should move on, with or without a good deal on Abyei.

Furthermore, SPLM's negotiatory methodology on Abyei was

---

80   Douglas H. Johnson, *Abyei, the CPA and the war in Sudan new South*

81   *Ibid*

completely unsuccessful. Separating Abyei from the whole set of South Sudan's agenda and putting it with that of Nuba and Funj was injudicious. Abyei people's position was apparently different. Since the Addis Ababa Agreement, people of Abyei wanted their area to be reinstated to Southern Sudan, regardless of whether Sudan remains united or divided, but the other two areas wanted their grievances to be addressed within the whole context of the Sudanese political question (New Sudan). National Congress Party's leaders understood the dynamics and how the international community works, hence continued to intransigently veto whatever motion related to Abyei, starting from the rejection of ABC Experts' report which claimed to have exceeded their mandate up to Abyei referendum which was slated to be conducted concurrently with the referendum of Southern Sudan.

Peace brokers' principal focus was to end the civil war, but they were less concerned with postbellum issues. Abyei Protocol was Washington's byproduct imposed on the parties, but international guarantors were too credulous to believe that SPLM and NCP would, in good will, elect to cooperate in implementing it without a third party's pressure! Lack of institutions and mechanisms for monitoring and evaluation with powers to impose compliance was the chief cause of failure.

Moreover, Kiir led SPLM's position on Abyei was varied, hence Abyei Protocol was utterly conned according to NCP helmsmen's will. It is now thirteen years since South Sudan gained independence, yet the issue of Abyei is moving nowhere.

Governments of Sudan and South Sudan had been consciously avoiding anything that may cause them to collide. As a result,

Abyei's file was jettisoned and considered a vexatious matter. This took some people to defensively conclude that Abyei's issue was not stalemated because of an insoluble disagreement over it between Sudan and South Sudan, but the interlinked systems in Khartoum and Juba agreed to disagree in order to furtively continue sucking its oil as precisely stated below.

> "Abyei remains in a political stalemate. This impasse has been politically productive for Juba and Khartoum; even if the conflict in Sudan had not broken out on 15 April, it is unlikely that any progress would have been made with regard to the territory's future. A decade of diplomatic stalemate has been deleterious to the people of Abyei, but eminently productive for Sudan. Khartoum benefits from oil revenues from Diffra, which, despite the commitments made in several peace agreements, do not go to Abyei, but are instead shared with Juba." [82]

Abyei's file had been archived since 2013 by the agglutinate systems in Khartoum and Juba to allow their factotums to successfully handle the issues of their mutual concerns. After huge pressure exerted by some actors in the international community on Sudan, President Salva Kiir Mayardit and Omar al Bashir met in early January 2013, in Addis Ababa. The latter imposed his country's will by unnecessarily tying the conduct of Abyei referendum

---

82   *Attacks from both sides; Abyei existential dilemma*/July 2023/ Dr. Joshua Craze

with establishment of a joint administration, a demand which the people of Abyei rejected up to the time of writing. In a nutshell, Abyei had never been a matter of genuine contest between Kiir's Administration and Sudan, but Ngok and Sudan. I am utterly convinced that President Kiir's unforgettable coterie of advisors, the likes of Bona Malwal Madut, Martin Elia Lomoro, Tut Gatluak Manime among others were arguably co-authors of Abyei's political misfortune, particularly, after the independence of Southern Sudan.

It is therefore, significant for the generation of South Sudanese leaders which will succeed the current tyrannical, confused system to fathom the nature of Abyei's political issue, then genuinely work for the realisation of its final status.

As I mentioned elsewhere in this book, Abyei issue had stuck neither because of political vagueness, nor legal inapplicableness, but National Congress Party took advantage of Kiir Administration's undulate stand on Abyei. The last genuine diplomatic attempt to unlock the stalemate on Abyei was the African Union High Implementation Panel's proposal (AUHIP), popularly known as Mbeki's Proposal. On 21 September 2012, the AUHIP entrusted by the African Union's Peace and Security Council (AUPSC) tabled a proposal in which mechanisms were outlined for the resolution of Abyei's final status. This proposal provided for the people of Abyei to vote on a referendum in October 2013.

Regarding the problem of voter eligibility, President Mbeki, the head of AUHIP resolved that; seasonal migrants are not eligible for voting, only permanent settlers of Abyei area, the Ngok Dinka. That was what came in his advice to President Bashir of

Sudan and Salva Kiir Mayardit of South Sudan on 17 October 2012. However, the AUPSC accepted the proposal on 24 October 2012, and described it as a fair, equitable and workable solution for the dispute. All the regional bodies entrusted with tutelaric roles, African Union's Peace and Security Council, IGAD and all their operative mechanisms were still supportive of the Abyei political cause, but Sudan managed to get away using its sovereignty and suzerainty over South Sudan, while President Kiir, affected by political hangovers, cringed as if he was a governor of a region under Sudan.

Given the current political status in the Republic of Sudan, it is very hard to prevision a resolution for the issue of Abyei that could be mutually brought about by Sudan and South Sudan in the near future. Sudan is standing on a precipice, prima facie, it is breaking up. It is up to Kiir's Administration, or any political system that would follow to continue this negative *laissez-faire* policy on Abyei and wait for decades until Khartoum re-gains its political health, or take a bold step towards a resolution of Abyei Area's final status.

It is contrary to universal political understanding to ease up on such an inimical country and wait for her re-stablisation in order to resolve territorial disputes such as Abyei, Kafia Kenji and Panthau! Khartoum had, since independence of Southern Sudan, been manipulating Juba's full economic reliance on oil which most infrastructures are in its territories. Now it is getting worse as Sudan has been practically divided between the warring parties and each may claim sovereignty or control over (x) and (y) of the oil facilities. This card (oil) which Khartoum had been scaring

Juba with, is no more effective after it became non-operational. However, it is arguably believed that Abyei is, and will not be a priority for any of the two parties (SAF & RSF).

Furthermore, the centre of power in Sudan is under remaking, which could end with a birth, rebirth of new sociopolitical entities or even a new country. Henceforth, Misseriya shall no longer continue to be a preferred *political toddler* in the region of Kordofan.

In light of this opaque political picture in Sudan and South Sudan, Ngok people of Abyei, the actual stakeholders who had been put through the mill, should cease political dependency, grasp a space for themselves to be party to, and have a louder, unskippable say on the question of their political destiny. While trekking towards the final status, let all be mindful and thoughtful of the ultimate sacrifices made by Ngok's great men and women for Abyei to be in this unmistakable position in the history of South Sudan's struggle for freedom. Despite the enormous, disproportionate conditions, let the revolution's sparkle remains vivacious, and bear in mind that

the darkest hour is before the dawn.

APPENDIX

Date : 3rd/Feb/2023.

Hon . Lt. Gen. Koul Diem Koul. Chief Administrator, Abyei Special
Administrative Area, Abyei.

Subject : <u>Great Concern Over Continuous Abyei force occupation of Twic lands in Warrap
state of former Bahr Al Gazal Province.</u>

We the undersigned persons are members of Transitional National legislature, who are very
much concerned over continuous force occupation of Twic lands before and currently under
your administrative management.

So many Twic citizens and other citizens from greater Gogrial died in the occupied areas of Twic
County alloted Agok place as a camp for Ngok Dinka IDPs, now forcely occupied by Abyei
Administration in form of civil administration and security forces.

The borders you claimed as coming from Hague are strange and not known to Warrap, and
Twic people who are the actual owners of the lands.

What we know is the dispute between Abyei and messieryia of Muglad over latitude 13 degree
border within former Kordufan that took them to Hague for arbitration together with
unfortunate case of Panthou of Ruweng of former Unity State from former Upper Nile Province
that finally got lost to former Kordufan of Sudan in Hague arbitration in total absence of the
real owners of the land, that is the current Adminitrative Area of Ruweng. This is not going to
happen to Twic land whose people defended this dear land by sacrificing their lives through
many generations to secure this very land for their children to live in confortably togther with
their brothers and sisters of South Sudan.

Twic County is not a party to the Abyei arbitration because they were not there in Hague Court
of Arbitration.

Abyei is part of former Kordufan province now known as Southern Kordofan province and any
talks of borders between South Sudan and Sudan are governed by borders of 1st January 1956

of nine provinces when Sudan took independence to which Abyei was being administered in Southern Kordofan province. Your reference to Governors' conference for setltlement can be acceptable as a go in between factor for this case because the current dispute between Warrap state or Twic County are fasisely shown as Sudan lands in Southern Kordufan for which you are the prime instruments to acquire Twic lands using borders of former Southern Kordufan mapping to include Twic lands inside the borders on 1st January 1956 before Abyei arbitration is settled to promote the validity of these lands as belonging to Abyei of former Kordufan province that borders former Bahr El Ghazal Province as they stood on 1st January 1956 Independence.It is a crafty game that will never see a finished house.

We are following all those crafty make ups of mechanical borders buildings under secret discussions to annex Twic lands to the so called Abyei Box. Therefore the Council of State cannot settle this issue in the asbsence of 1st January 1956 borders with Sudan. This is our prime document never to be ignored by any body who has people of South Sudan at heart to do wrong decision that would make South Sudanese to engage in conflict over a clear case favouring former Bahr El Ghazal Province that is Twic County. Anything short of this would not be acceptable as it happened to people of Ruweng. Our borders with former Kordufan province to which you are attached, are governed by Comprehensive Peace Agreement (CPA) that adopted and agreed to the 1st January 1956 for borders settlement between Sudan and South Sudan without excluding Abyei as you appear to project or believe.

The issue of Abyei Box is your own drawn up maps with friendly NGOs we know. Such self drawn up maps as remarked by H. E the President of the Republic in the Governors' conference that such maps drawn by NGOs, are not officially recognized by South Sudan government because they have not passed through any legal channels of the government like Parliament, Executive so that they become legal instruments gazetted and consequently be recognized internationally. In the absence of these processes your claim of international recognition is self proclaim recognition and have nowhere to be honored for application due to lack of legal ground.

Your recent attempt to encroach into Aweil lands using UNISFA tool was repulsed with great force by the citizens there because you were a stranger that have no borders with Aweil but you were trying to make expansion of your new empire into the lands of others after you lost your lands to the friendly neighbours in former Kordufan Province.

It is Twic County that has borders with Aweil due to long historical ties between the two communities during the wars of Turkco Egyptian Sudan and the Mahdia. Ngok Dinka people were not party to those wars but living peacefully together with Arabs of Messeiryia and the Nuba. This is history we all know in greater Gogrial, Ruweng, Northern Sudan and Chieftaincy of the nine Ngok Dinka sections.

UNISFA presence south of River Kiir is totally illegal and we advise you to relocate them north of River Kiir together with the administration to avoid any conflict to the disadvantage of the two communities. We always said in some of the letters we wrote that those Ngok Dinka who are still feeling insecure to go to the North of River Kiir can remain under administration of Twic county in the camp of Agok; but nobody from you is ready to talk. All our appeals have at all times fallen into deaf ears of powerful Abyei elites.

Hon. chief, the best way of coming out when you are seriously entangled into a problem is to take courageous stand to tell the truth. Our people have suffered very much in the hands of your authorities before you came in and now as we talk about humiliation of our people in their own lands under Abyei force occupation without just cause. You will be embarrassed when these stories of killings, mistreatments and wrong detentions by your authorities inside Twic lands by Abyei Administrators, are unveiled for possible case litigations.

Those maps which you Ngok elites drew inside Twic lands will not see light because they are crafty and baseless. When Akonoon of Mareeng section agreed with Jok to prepare the present structure of Ngok Dinka settlements along north of the River Kiir as a base facing settlement towards the north; the two agreed that Jok of Padhieu and leader of Abior section go together with his sections or clans to the western side facing Keregi or Kerega to the north. While Akonoon of Dhiendior or Mareeng section together with his other sections like Dill go to eastern side along north of River Kiir facing Nuba mountains to the north and Ruweng to the east. The rest of Ngok Dinka sections were settled between the two leaders except Bongo that was left in the extreme north at their original settlement. The rest of the sections settled in between the two leaders strutures to the west and east that borders Ruweng to the east along north of River Kiir and Twic South of River Kiir to Ruweng and Ngok generally.

To the extreme west of Twic settlement is Thon Ayuel Longar bordering Aweil way from the South to the north of River Kiir where they have border with Arabs Hamr together with Riiny Twic sections of Liangarol, Goi, Aruet and Hol up to Bar Ajak historical side. These are historical proofs that will engage all of us if matters go too far from now as they are being driven at moment.

Our people have suffered enough in their own land as a result of the land given to Ngok Dinka to shelter in as displaced persons when Turalei could not carry Ngok and those of Turalei over services at Turalei air strip which is well known to Comrade Monydhaang when he was the very commissioner who was there when comrade Deng Aloor Kuol came to Turalei in 2002 as Governor of Greater Bahr El Ghazal to arrange with the Commissioner of Twic County to allot a piece of land for the Internal Displaced Persons from Abyei of former Kordufan Province. This place was Agok of sub chief Teeng Akoi of Kuac Anganya of chieftaincy of Amuol Twic Section that was chosen to shelter them for better services through airstrip of their own. Now totally denied by you and possibly by ALL Ngok people despite the good intensions for which it was done by late James Yol Kuol Bol who was the Commissioner of Twic county witnessed by some of us, no regret on our side for your denial for good offers of our land to shelter your internal displaced persons at times of difficulties getting rewarded with stone now.

Let us observe good neighbourhood and avoid conspiracies, bullying, mockery. Killings and wars being chased by your side all the way from the war of liberation until today. Let us NOT endanger the lives of our people.

The claim you made that Agok was declared as county of Ngok HGrs in Chukudum SPLM National Liberation Council meeting appears to suggest that Twic people were not there at the time of the declaration. Since Twic members of the Movement were not there as it is implicit in your talks; produce the document to that effect and the Chairman of that meeting, because any meeting chaired by John Garang would not exclude Twic members and this development could have not passed without reaction of Twic Leaders. It is your own invention.

The action of the commissioner of Twic County writing directly to your authority was influenced by us as MPs of the area to timely correct the insecurity you suddenly stepped up through illegal survey of Twic lands as an emergency to stop any insecurity that may engage the two communities into violence. It is your action that can be described as contributing factor in generating conflict and violence and you will be implicated in this long manufacturing of problems over and over again by All Administrators of Abyei. It remains to be seen how future will judge our behaviours towards each others given the way our people have suffered in the hands of your administration inside Abyei Headquarters and in their own lands at Agok Camp with the view to subdue them accept your administration as legal entity in their land.

All the good call of the commissioner without using any violence still remain valid and we repeat again to your good offices to relocate your illegal administration and UNISFA now occupying Twic county land for death to go to Abyei HQrs . If we are to remain in good relationships as it used to be between the two communities, let us promote good

This ends our sincere letter to your honorable authorities

Signed:

1-Hon. Charles Majak Aleer Deng.

2-Hon. Dr Majok Yak Majok

3-Hon. Victoria Adhar Arop.

4-Hon. Justice Angier Ring.

5-Hon.Nyadeng Malek Dielic.

11-Hon. Elisabeth Acuei Yol.

12-Hon. Ayen Luka Ngor

13-Hon. Mayom Kuoc Malek

14-Hon. Nyadeng Kerubino Kuanyin

15-Hon. Albino Mathem Ayuel.

16-Hon. Chan Malual Chan

17-Hon. Joseph Mabior Malek Arop

18-Hon. Goc Makuac Mayol

19-Hon. Kuot Atoc Thokluoi

Copies:

1 .H. E Salva Kiir Mayardit , President of the Republic of South Sudanese.

2.H.E Dr. Riek Macher Teny, 1st Vice President for Governance Cluster.

3.H. E Wani Egga Vice President for economic cluster .

4.H. E Taban Deng Gai Vice President for Infrastructure.

5.H.E Hussein Abdel Bagi Ayii Akol for Serrvice Cluster.

JOK ALOR BULABEK

6.H.E Nyndeng Garang De Mabior Vice President for Gender, Youth and Sport Cluster.

7. Rt. Hon. Nunu Kumba,
Speaker of the legislature

8. Honorable Deng Deng Akoon, Deputy Speaker of the legislature .

9. Hon. Tut Galuak,
Security Affairs Adviser.

10. Hon. Lt. Gen. Aleu Ayieny Aleu,
Governor, Warrap State.

11. Hon. Lt. Gen. Obote Mamur,
Minister of Security Affairs. Office of the President.

12.Hon. Lt. Gen. Mahmoud Solomon Agook, Minister of interior

13. Hon. Mayik Ayii Deng,
Minister of Foreign affairs and International8 Cooperation.

14.National Security

16.Hon. Engineer Deng Tong Goc,
Commissioner,

Republic of South Sudan

The Presidency

Abyei Special Administrative Area

Chief Administrator's Office

Ref: RSS/ASAA/C.A.O/L/03/2022   Date: 31ˢᵗ January, 2022

To: Hon. Lt. Gen. Aleu Ayieny Aleu,

   Governor of Warrap State;

   Kuajok.

Dear Comrade,

Sub: Letter of Protest

I am writing in protest to Hon. Eng. Deng Goch Tong, the Commissioner of Twic County, letter No. RSS/WSK/CO/50.A.1 dated 14/12/2021, attached below, addressed to the Abyei Area Chief Administrator, in which he intensively used strange, non-institutional and unjustified harsh language, without respect to my leadership position or even the historical ties that have been linking the two communities' leadership and the grassroot levels throughout our history.

This letter has raised multiple concerns in contravention of all official correspondence exigencies known in every institution, a reason which necessitates reacting to it in a way or another and I found the best option is writing to you and not responding to him. I would like therefore to highlight the following:

   (1) It would have been procedural and advisable that such a letter to come directly from Warrap State Governor and not from him.
   (2) Such contentious issues like the ones the Commissioner raised Hon. Governor, are normally discussed face-to-face by the leadership to avoid possible inconveniences in the interest of the stakeholders concerned and not in the way these issues were raised.

Hon. Governor;

The points that were raised by the Commissioner should not be left without reaction, therefore, I would like to briefly react as follows:

   (1) He talks about Agok, Athony and a place he named Mijak Deng Muon illegal survey by saying "I instruct your administration to immediately stop and relocate to Abyei HQs north of River Kiir". This is what I called strange, non-institutional and unjustified harsh language from a constitutional post holder, who is supposed to be well informed and knowledgeable about government hierarchy system.

(2) The Commissioner also added Hon. Governor that, Agok Town became a IDPs center in 2002 – 2003 when late Gen. James Yol Kuol, hosted the Ngok Dinka IDPs over there, and this to me is just a corrupted history, because the SPLM/SPLA history defeats his claim as we all know that Agok was named as Abyei County Headquarters in June 1994, during the SPLM First National Convention held in Chukudum.

(3) As you are aware Hon. Governor, the States' boundaries disputes, were the most contentious issues reported by Hon. Governors in the 5th Governors' Forum, being the root causes of the inter and intra communal conflicts and the Forum recommends in its recommendation No. (9) which says "the Council of States to actively resolve inter and intra- states boundary' conflicts and between states and administrative areas", therefore it is advisable that all of us should adhere to this recommendation in letter and spirit.

(4) The Commissioner has instructed me to immediately relocate UNISFA from south of River Kiir northward, and my reaction to this point is that, UNISFA is in the area as per (SOFA) the Status of Forces Agreement between the Republic of South Sudan and UN. This point looks odd and unreasonable..!!.

(5) Six (6) Ngok Dinka Chiefdoms in three (3) counties, have their presence south of River Kiir namely: Dhiil, Manyuar, Mareng, Anyiel, Achueng and Abior since time immemorial in Rum-Amer, Mijak and Alal Counties, these indigenous communities are asked to remain in their homelands under Twic County protection or choose to go to Abyei North of River Kiir Hon. Governor by the Commissioner. This is a very strange request of its kind to dictate on the rightful owners of a certain land to remain under your protection or face the consequences by chasing them out of their home areas.

(6) Abyei Area borders had been internationally well defined by The Hague Arbitration and all the areas the Commissioner indicated in his letter fall within Abyei Box, therefore are not contested area; and if he has a different view, then it is advisable for him to compile and present his new historical documents and evidences to the Council of States for settlement.

(7) The Abyei Box map is internationally agreed upon and recognized by the Government of the Republic of South Sudan, and H.E. the President of the Republic of South Sudan, used it as a reference for the Establishment Order of Abyei Special Administrative Area in February 2015, and Rum-Amer, Mijak and Alal Counties were therefore established Legally.

(8) The Commissioner also advised me Hon. Governor to order UNISFA Mission to adhere to its initial mandate and relinquish the current incursion south of River Kiir and as you know Hon. Governor, this is solely within H.E the President prerogative or Ministry of Foreign Affairs and not within my capacity for sure.

(9) The Commissioner language and behavior pose a clear threat of violence in Abyei Area, therefore he is to be held responsible should anything of this kind occurred.

(10) He is calling on us to observe Abyei Protocol, a task which we are practically doing on the ground by virtue of our responsibilities.

Hon. Governor;

In conclusion, at different stages some honest leaders have exerted efforts to reduce the emerging and sporadic tensions, while others insist on the intrusion of their personal agenda on our two communities' relations and these elements are mainly government officials and political leaders. The populace are innocent.

Ngok and Twic Communities are one people in two State, who are peacefully living together in their respective home areas and villages, therefore fostering the spirit of peaceful coexistence, repudiating all forms of frictions, antagonism and such unnecessary skirmishes on the boundaries issues, can be settled by the Council of States.

As the two communities' leadership, our priority is to propose effective crisis management mechanisms to all contentious issues as well as ensuring peaceful solutions and not widening cleavages between our communities.

The Commissioner labeled numerous unsubstantiated accusations against the Abyei Area Administration which is not advisable and the tone of threat and harsh language he used in his letter, is paradoxically not compatible with the peace call in his conclusion, therefore he should be disciplined to put to an end such a blatant transgression.

Please, Honorable Governor, accept the assurances of my highest consideration and Regards.

Thanks

Yours Sincerely,

Signed:—

Hon. Lt. Gen. Kuol Deim Kuol,

Chief Administrator,

Abyei Special Administrative Area,

Abyei Town.

Cc: H.E. President of the Republic of South Sudan

Cc: Director General of National Security Services- ISB

Cc: Abyei File Office

Cc. File

Republic of South Sudan

Council of States

Report on communal conflict between
Ngok of Abyei and Twic of Warrap

Prepared by the Ad Hoc committee formed
by the Council of States to investigate the
causes of the conflict

Fact established from documents, findings
of committee, observations, solutions
provided by the two sides to the conflict,
recommendations and conclusion

March 3rd 2022 – February 22nd 2023

ABR

- Facts established from the documents provided by Warrap State and Abyei Administrative Area and presentation of the Hon. Governor, Chief Administrator and the Hon. National Minister of Interior

1. The Committee found out that the letter written on the 3rd /Feb/2022 by the members of the National Legislature representing Warrap State, Twic County in particular, which stressed that the boundary between Kordofan and Bahr El Ghazal or Abyei and Twic is as it stood at 1/1/1956, as came in the CPA on the resolution of Abyei (page 2) is one of the root causes.

2. The Ad hoc Committee established that the objections made by the Hon. Members of the Legislature representing Warrap State, Twic County, on Abyei box that it is because it was drawn by the NGOs is not true, because the Abyei box was drawn by the Hague Arbitration and the ruling was highly welcome by the government of the Republic of South Sudan and Sudan. Therefore, the claim made by the members of National Legislature representing Twic County on the speech of the President in the governors' forum about Abyei box, which they have mentioned in their letter page 2, is totally contrary to the Presidential order No. 03/2015 for the establishment of Abyei Special Administrative Area, in the box as it is attached in the order (2) Feb/18/2018 sub-order (a) see annex No. 3.14

3. The Committee found out that the Honorable members' letter contains words of threat against Abyei Administration and inciting Twic community to fight for their right (page 2 the second last paragraph and page 3 and 2nd paragraph). See annex 3.6

4. The Committee also found that the honorable members of National Legislature representing Twic, made incitement by influencing Hon. Eng. Deng Tong Goch, the commissioner of Twic County to write a direct letter to the Chief Administrator of Abyei in an insubordination to his superior, the Hon. governor of

1

ABR

Warrap State as came in their letter (page 4 paragraphs 4 and five 5) when they said for the smooth relationship of the two communities, you have to relocate your illegal administration of Abyei and UNISFA to the North River Kiir. This instigation was also alluded to by Hon. Aleu Ayeny in his presentation to the Council of States on the 3rd/March/2022 (point b page 4 paragraphs 2, 3, and 4) that he said the letter written by Turalei County Commissioner was a ''wanton provocation of the Abyei Administration and typical insubordination to the Governor of Warrap State'' end of quote. See annex 3.5

5. The Ad hoc Committee established that there was belligerent tune raised by honorable members representing Twic such as: Hon. Charles Majak Aleer, Hon. Majok Yak Majok and Hon. Dr. Kuany Mayom Deng, when they asked that what the hell is Abyei administration doing? The honorable members said if the following steps are not taken care of, the tension between the two communities shall not be prevented: relocation of (1. UNISFA 2. Agok and Athony to be put under the administration of Warrap State 3. Abyei IDPs should go to the North River Kiir 4. UNMMIS to replace UNISFA in Agok 5. Conduct of the reconciliation between Twic and Ngok Dinka (paragraphs 5 and 6).

6. The Committee found that the map attached to uncle. Bona Malual's Book titled ''Abyei of Ngok Dinka Not Yet South Sudan'' shows the boundary of 1/1/1956 clearly at the South of river Kiir adjacent to the box. See annex 3.15

7. The Committee found that the first attacked was carried out on 10-26/Feb/2022 as come in the presentation of the Hon. Chief Administrator of Abyei (point No.9 page 5), Hon. Governor of Warrap State, when he said that on 10/Feb/2022 (paragraph 6 page 4) that the Twic youth took the law into their hands by attacking Agok area, Hon. Mahmood Solomon Agok, the National Minister of Interior, also confirm it in his

2

report to the plenary as well as it was confirmed by UNISFA and Twic and Ngok communities. see annex 3.2

8. The Committee found that the Communities along the borders are too ignorant on the 1/1/1956 boundary between Kordufan and Bahr El Ghazal as well as between Abyei Special Administrative Area and Warrap State, where by both communities of Ngok and Twic are saying that their boundary is in accordance to 1/1/1956, but if they are asked that where is 1/1/1956 practically? Twic said it is exactly inside the river Kiir and Ngok said it is inside the river Alaal at the far South of river Kiir. See annex 3.17

- **Findings of the Ad hoc Committee from the executive of Warrap State and Abyei Administrative Area, parliamentarians, women, youth, chiefs, UNISFA, UNMMIS, business community, individuals, Twic community in Abyei, civil society and Agok/Anet area meetings**

1. The Committee found out that Ngok and Twic Dinka are known to be peaceful neighbors for Centuries, after they had migrated to the presence territories of Abyei Special Administrative Area and Warrap State, but some exceptional social frictions/skirmishes has also been there.

2. **The Committee established that Agok area was there before 1997 as claimed by Twic community that they gave it out to Ngok through the request of late. Dr. John** Garang is not verifiable simply, because: a. Somesay it was given to Ngok in 1994, 1997, 1998, 2002, 2003 and 2004 b. The conditions set out by Twic community to give out their land to Ngok as requested from them by Dr. John Garang are not traceable (documentations) c. Internal Displaced Persons (IDPs) cannot be given a land of more than 60 kilometers squares, whatsoever the case.

3

ABK

3. The Committee found out that **Twic wants UNISFA** to relocate to the North side of river Kiir in 2022 while UNISFA was deployed in Agok area since 2011, as a result of the court of Arbitration/Hague ruling.

4. **The Committee found that Twic community wanted** to be paid land rents by Gen. Ping Deng and Kur Ajing for their farms which they have established since 2015.

5. **The Committee established that** the fighting between Kuac of Twic and Diil and Anyiel of Ngok Dinka in 1945 was the one led the two sections of Ngok to cross to the North of river Kiir as claimed by **Sultan. Jacob, Madhal Lang**

6. **The Committee was not able to establish the claimed made by the Hon. Deng Deng,** that the State government was directed not to take any measures about the conflict and when he was asked who directed the State authority not to take any action to stop the conflict? Then he failed to answer.

7. **The Committee found that the dismissal of Hon. Biar Biar, the former commissioner of Turalei County by the Warrap State Legislative Assembly, according Hon. Nyanyai Riak and Hon. Achuai Arop,** that it was because he went and carried out the demarcation of land in Agok area without being authorized.

8. **The Committee found that the information given to the Committee in Turalei County on 30/10/2022, by Twic (specifically by Mrs. Achai Mangar) that seven (7) people were burned alive by Ngok in Abyei, the same day the committee was meeting women group in Turalei, was properly crosscheck and verified by the Committee, but it was found out that it was not true.**

9. **The Committee crosscheck the information given by Mrs. Aluel Aguek Noui (Aweng Payam) and Mrs. Adior Nyol Riak (Turalei Payam, Turalei County) that Gen. Ping Deng Kuol was on the ground commanding the forces fighting against**

Twic, this was also verified by the Committee and found out that it was not true.

10.   The Committee found that the information provided by Mrs. Abuk Chan Bol, that there were Twic inside UNISFA, the committee verified it and found out that it is true, there were nine (9) members of Twic under UNISFA protection, whom were accused by their colleagues from Ngok that they were carrying out some wild information on social media and used to give out some vital information to their brothers in Turalei to come and attacked Ngok in Agok area.

11.   The Committee found out that there are no "pols" but boundary coordinates provided by the court in 2009 to the government of South Sudan and Sudan, according to Gen. Kuol Diem Kuol, the Chief Administrator of Abyei Special Administrative Area. These coordinates are with the two Engineers: a. Kuol Biong b. Riing Kuol Arop.

12.   The Committee found that Maj. Gen. Akuei Ajou Akuei, Maj. Gen. Makal Kuol Deng and Brig. Gen. Chol Madol, the commanders of battalion 7b and taskforce stationed in Agok by the Vice President for Services Cluster have gravely contributed to the conflict by allowing the army to participate in the communal conflict between Ngok and Twic Dinka.

13.   The Committee found out that the visit of Dr. John Garang, Gen. Salva Kiir, Dr. Riek Machar, Dr. Lam Akol, Gen. Kuol Manyang Juuk and etc in 2004 to Agok area, reception was organized by Ngok not Twic and 12 Bulls were slaughtered. These twelve (12) Bulls signified the followings: a. nine (9) Bulls for Nine Ngok Dinka Chiefdoms b. one Bull for the visitors c. one Bull for Abyei County and d. one Bull for Abiemnom IDPs hosted in Agok by Ngok.

22.   The Committee established that the cessation of hostilities signed in Aweil by the two communities initiated by the High-Level Committee led by VP, H.E, Hussein Abdel Bag, lacks implementation and monitoring mechanisms for it to hold water and that was why it was violated in the next day of its signature by the two conflicting communities.

23.   The Committee found out that the books written by **Uncle. Bona Malual Madut and Uncle. Dr. Francis DengMading** are assumed by the two conflicting communities that they are the prime causes to the current communal violence of Twic and Ngok Dinka. See annex 3.15 and 3.16

24.   **The Committee found that the communities along the boundary line of 1/1/1956 and other internal borders are so ignorant on 1/1/1956 boundary coordinates** left by the British. Where by the two communities of Ngok and Twic are saying that their boundary is in accordance to 1/1/1956, but if they are asked that where is 1/1/1956 practically? Twic said it is exactly inside river Kiir and Ngok said it is at river Alaal at the far South of river Kiir.

25.   The Committee found that the Government of Warrap State has never taken any measures to stop the conflict and it has left Twic youth astray to decide and mobilized one another toward the war. (See testimony of Hon. Deng Deng, Twic representative in Warrap State Legislative Assembly)

26.   The Committee established the fact that there was no targeting killing against Twic in Abyei or Agok, the people of Twic who ran away from Abyei were just fearing from unknown as said by UNISFA and Twic community in Abyei as well.

27.   The Committee found that the Tiger battalion, a new force deployed to Agok area which has already arrived is occupying the schools, hospitals, residentials areas, government institutions and the markets

28.	The Committee found out that there is need for the deployment of SSPDF in **Ajakuac and Mayen-Abun Payams of Turalei County, in** order to monitor the activities of the armed youth from both sides who may be in a position to attack each other.

29.	The Committee established that Hon. Aleu Ayeny, governor of Warrap State admitted that he was misled by the politicians, when he entered Agok with his Gubernatorial flag flying and thereafter he apologies to the Hon. Chief Administrator of Abyei Special Administrative Area,

30.	The Committee found out that lack of communication between the Chief Administrator of Abyei Special Administrative Area and Warrap State Governor had negatively intensified the conflict between the two sisterly communities.

31.	The Committee found out that the boundary line is not running inside river Kiir as claimed by Twic, but run parallel to river Kiir at far south in the periodic swampy area of Alaal as it is in July/1955 and 1/1/1956 maps. See map of Sudan survey July/1955 annex 3.15

32.	The Committee found out that the Letter written by the Hon. Kon Manyiel Kuol, the former governor of Twic State to H.E, Gen. Salva Kiir Mayardit, the President of the Republic of South Sudan, on January/30/2018, that if the Abyei box is not corrected then, it shall cause clans/communal conflict over some areas at South of river Kiir at any time. (Paragraph 4 page 4) is one of the incitements for Twic community to fight against Ngok community. See annex 3.4

33.	**The Committee established** that the testimony of Mr. Achuil Malith that Diil section of Ngok Dinka has land south river Kiir bordering Kuac Anganya and that in 2010 election Diil and Kuac Anganya have one constituency represented by Hon. Arop Madut

www.ingramcontent.com/pod-product-compliance
Lightning Source LLC
Chambersburg PA
CBHW011745020426
42333CB00022B/2715